In This Issue

PIVOT MAGAZINE

Founder
Jason Miller

President
Juddene Villarin

Web Master
Joel Phillips

Designs
ReliableStaffSolutions.com

Copyright © 2025 PIVOT

ISBN: 978-1-957217-94-9

Contact
Jason Miller
Founder
1151 Eagle Drive #345
Loveland, CO 80537
jason@strategicadvisorboard.com

Shelby Jo Long
Editor-in-Chief
shelby@strategicadvisorboard.com
877-944-0944

From the Editor

Signal Over Noise

This issue is about cutting through the noise and not just being heard, but being trusted.

Authority is changing. Influence is no longer about volume or visibility. It is about clarity, credibility, and the courage to lead with substance when others are chasing trends. Whether you are navigating the rise of AI voices, working across borders, or building a brand beyond the algorithm, one thing is clear: what worked before no longer guarantees relevance.

Inside these pages, we dive deep into what it takes to lead today. To grow with intention. To show up as a founder, a strategist, a team builder, or a creator who understands that trust is the only thing that compounds.

In a world of constant distraction, the leaders who will thrive are the ones who choose depth over hype.

Shelby Jo Long
Editor-in-Chief

From the Desk
Of The President

Rewriting the Playbook

There is a shift happening and this issue names it.

Consumers are walking away from influencer culture. Teams are redefining what collaboration looks like. Founders are asking whether the price of growth is worth their freedom. And everywhere you look, the question of trust is front and center.

This issue was created to answer those questions not with gimmicks, but with grounded insights. From AI's impact on credibility to the resurgence of the generalist, we are spotlighting leaders who are building real authority in a distracted world.

Ask yourself:

- What kind of influence are you really building
- What part of your work still depends on borrowed attention
- Are you leading in a way that earns trust, not just engagement

This is not just a shift in tactics. It is a shift in mindset.

Let us lead with clarity. Let us build what outlasts the trends.

JUDDENE VILLARIN *J. V.*

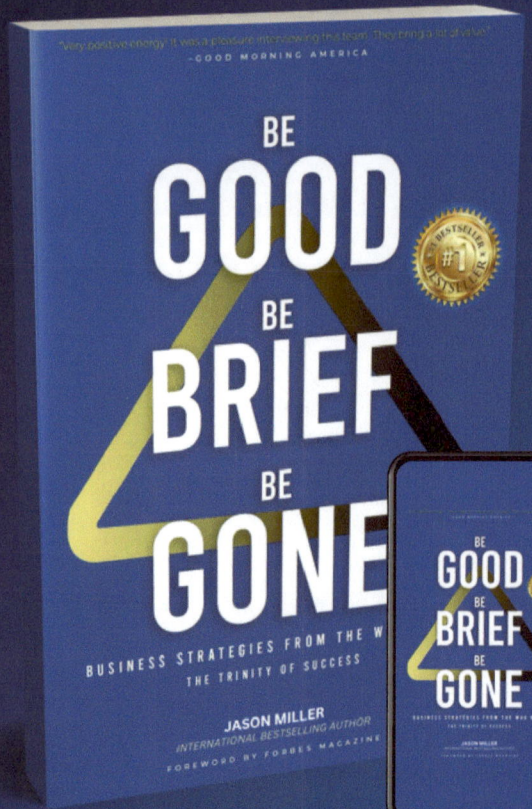
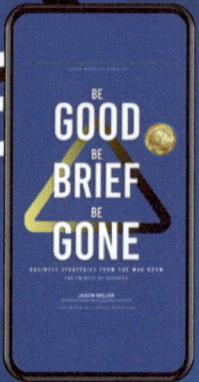

Influence Without Noise

Building Authority in a Distracted World

Noise doesn't silence you. Conformity does. The moment you stop echoing what everyone else is saying, your voice finally stands out.

When the volume of voices rises each moment, being heard isn't enough. Being remembered is the real win. So let's dive into how you can forge real authority without turning into a megaphone in a marketplace full of static.

Cutting Through the Static

Imagine you're at a concert. The band's playing, the crowd's cheering... but you're behind a wall of speakers and a roaring fanbase. You want to stand out.

The same applies to your professional field. Everyone's posting, speaking, publishing but the challenge isn't simply to speak louder. It's to speak distinctly.

In a distracted world, the signals you send must not only be consistent but strategically different. When everyone says, "Here's what you could do," you say: "Here's what you shouldn't do." When everyone offers "5 tips," you publish a manifesto, a contrarian stance, or a bold forecast. According to one analysis, part of true thought leadership is taking a unique stance that cuts through the noise.

Getting heard = being visible. Being remembered = being unforgettable.

Define Your Authority Zone

Before you go full-blast, you must anchor yourself into a "zone of authority."

- What topic do you actually own?

- What expertise do you bring that's hard to replicate?

- What lens do you view it through that's unique?

This is your niche. Without a niche, you're just "another voice." With one, you become the voice. As one article puts it: "Before you can establish yourself as a thought leader, it's crucial to define your niche and expertise."

Think of it this way: A lighthouse doesn't try to light up the whole horizon, just the channel. Your niche is the channel.

Action step: Write down one sentence: "I help [X] solve [Y] by [Z]".

X = the specific audience you serve
Y = the problem you address
Z = your unique method

From there, everything you publish, speak, or teach aligns with that sentence. That's how you build authority.

Create Content That Commands Attention

Here's where you roll up your sleeves. Authority isn't inherited, it's built. One of the critical pieces? High-quality content. But not just any content. Content with insight. Content that anticipates, disrupts, informs.

As one guide put it: "True thought leadership content... anticipates their future challenges and guides the conversation."

What does "commanding" content look like?

- It doesn't regurgitate. It innovates.

- It reflects your view of "what's next," not just "what is."

- It connects to your niche and offers actionable insight. Readers should walk away thinking: "I didn't know that. I need to act."

Formats to consider:

- In-depth articles (5,000+ words) that become reference pieces.

- Industry reports or original research-data elevates you.

- Podcast interviews or video sessions: your voice + your story.

- Micro-content for social that teases bigger work.

Tip: Use the "three-pillar" model:

- Industry Leadership – big picture, trend analysis.

- Personal Perspective – your story, your view.

- Actionable Insight – how the audience can act.

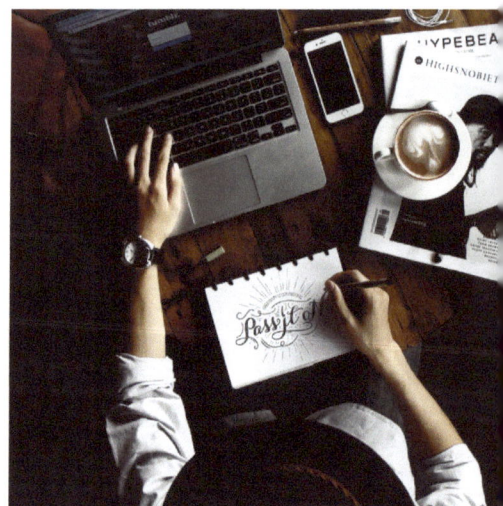

Consistency matters. You don't have to publish daily but you do have to show up, predictably. Over time, your audience starts looking for you.

Being Conversation-Worthily Authentic

There's a lot of hype about thought leadership. It's easy to mistake a big word count or flashy presentation for authority. But real authority is grounded in authenticity and credibility.

Here are the relational dynamics:

- Trust: Your audience must believe you know what you're talking about. That means backing claims with evidence, case-studies, or personal story.

- Transparency: Admit what you don't know or where you're still learning. That vulnerability often enhances relatability, rather than undermining your credibility.

- Engagement: Thought leadership isn't a monologue. It's part of a conversation. Respond to comments, invite discussion, and join community dialogues.

- Tone: We live in a distracted world. Readers log on expecting quick hits. That doesn't mean you dumb down your writing but you do need to be clear, accessible, compelling.

In short: Speak like a human, not like a press release.

Amplification Without the Megaphone

You've created meaningful, high-quality content. But how do you get it in front of the right people? This is where intelligent amplification comes into play.

What this means:

- Choose your platforms intentionally. If you're targeting corporate decision-makers, don't waste your energy on platforms with a youthful, consumer audience.

- Collaborate. Partner with industry peers, guest post on second-tier outlets, appear on podcasts—these moves vastly increase your reach.

- Use syndication smartly. Having your content appear in relevant media outlets lends validation and expands your footprint.

- Reuse intelligently. Your core idea can live in many formats: long-form article → LinkedIn carousel → Twitter thread → short video snippet. This keeps you present without reinventing the wheel.

Avoid: broadcasting everywhere just for the sake of volume. That dilutes your voice. Instead: pick fewer channels, own them, dominate them.

Differentiation Through a Bold Stance

Here's one of the hidden levers: You don't just want to be part of the conversation. You want to shape it. That means developing a point of view, a contrarian angle, a position that invites curiosity (and yes, sometimes discomfort).

As one article notes: "Identify what everyone in your industry accepts without question... then go public strategically with strong supporting evidence."

Why this matters:

- People gravitate toward voices that challenge them, not comfort them.

- You become known for that stance, not just your topic.

- Your authority becomes tied to your unique perspective, which is far harder to copy.

Examples could include:

- "The future of leadership is less about title and more about vulnerability"

- "Forget the customer is always right. Educate your customer first"

- "Growth hacking as you know it is dead, here's what replaces it"

When you take a stance, you attract people who align and, just as important, you repel those who don't. That's okay. Influence built on agreement isn't as strong as influence built on alignment.

Systems Over Spasms: Building for the Long Haul

Authority isn't built overnight. It's built by systems, not bursts.

Systemising your approach means:

- A clear content calendar: Map your themes, formats, platforms for 90 days +.

- Repurposing workflows: One research piece can become many content outputs across platforms.

- Engagement routines: Set aside time to respond, to follow up, to nurture community.

- Measurement: Track what's working- engagement, mentions, invitations, inbound leads. Make adjustments.

- Refreshing your viewpoint: The world changes fast. Stay curious and stay learning so your content remains relevant.

Imagine your authority like a garden. You plant seeds (ideas), water them (content), tend them (feedback & refinement), and over time you harvest (influence, reputation, opportunities). If all you do is show up once in a while to throw seeds randomly—you'll get patches of growth, but not a flourishing ecosystem.

Leverage Influence Ethically (Yes, That Matters)

In an age of distractions and noise, some shortcuts seem tempting - clickbait titles, viral gimmicks, sensationalism. But if you build your authority on that, you risk losing it faster than you gained it.

Real influence comes from ethical foundations:

- Never mislead. If you share data or claim expertise, make sure it's legit.

Why this matters:

- Give more than you take. Thought leadership isn't a sales pitch in disguise; it's service.

- Respect the audience. In a world full of noise, people prefer honesty and depth.

- Use your influence for impact. Once you have a voice, you have responsibility. Use it for direction, not just decoration.

In other words: Influence without integrity isn't real influence.

Building Authority in Highly Distracted Audiences

Because the world's attention span is shorter (hello, endless scroll), your strategies must reflect that reality.

Here's how to win attention without shouting:

- Lead with value: Start with what the audience gains—not "me, me, me."

- Use micro-moments: Short video clips, LinkedIn posts, stories. But always link them back to your broader mission.

- Signal clarity: Use headlines

and visuals that clearly communicate your niche and point of view - "This is about this, for this audience."

- Leverage timing: Publish when the topic is hot; ride the trend but anchor it to your unique viewpoint.

- Engage contextually: Don't just broadcast. Comment on others, respond in real time, become part of the conversation.

Because if you just show up at the megaphone, you blend into the crowd. But if you show up with precision, people actually notice.

From Authority to Influence: Translating Into Real Results

Building authority is only the beginning. The real payoff comes when that authority translates into influence and then into action - client engagements, industry partnerships, speaking invitations, demand generation.

Here's how to connect the dots:

- Authority → Recognition: People see you as credible.

- Recognition → Engagement: People start listening, responding, sharing.

- Engagement → Influence: People take action because of you.

- Influence → Impact: Your work leads to measurable results—opportunities, revenue, shift in perception.

This isn't linear and it may take time. But the framework is solid.

Don't forget measurement: Track your outcomes—mentions, citations, inbound requests, speaking offers. That helps you refine the strategy.

Pitfalls to Avoid

While you're building authority, watch out for these hazards:

- Generic content: Saying what everybody else says adds no value. Thought leadership demands fresh perspective.

- Inconsistency: Irregular output or shifting themes confuse your audience.

- Over-promotion: If everything you publish has a sales pitch, your audience tunes out.

- Ignoring feedback: Audience signals matter—if you're not listening, you'll miss your mark.

- No amplification strategy: Great content buried in the feed is wasted potential.

Your 90-Day Authority Sprint

Since you come from an execution background, let's make this practical.

Week 1-2

- Define your niche statement (X, Y, Z).

- Audit your existing content: what fits your authority zone, what doesn't.

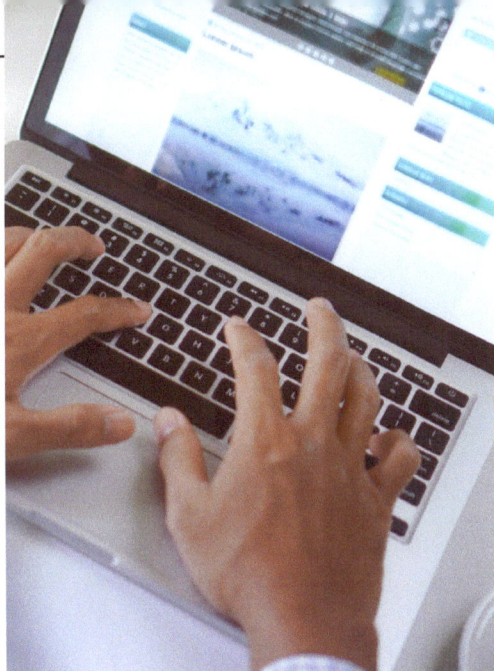

- Choose 3 primary channels (e.g., LinkedIn articles, podcast appearances, newsletter).

Week 3-6

- Create a flagship piece (e.g., 2,000+ word article, original research, or a bold viewpoint).

- Repurpose into supporting assets (social posts, short videos, infographic).

- Publish and engage in real time (reply to comments, join discussions).

Week 7-12

- Secure one partnership: a guest post, podcast interview, or collaboration.

- Measure early impact: views, shares, comments, inbound connections.

- Refresh your content and strategy based on what's resonating.

- Plan next quarter's calendar: themes, formats, cadences.

Beyond 90 days

- Use your systems: content reuse, amplification routines, feedback loops.

- Take a contrarian stance or elevate your viewpoint.

- Maintain consistency. Revisit niche and voice every six months to keep fresh.

Quiet Power Wins

We live in an era of noise but the loudest person isn't necessarily the most authoritative. The one who speaks clearly, with conviction, and with a distinct voice will build influence that lasts.

Here's your mindset shift:

- Don't aim to be heard by everyone. Aim to be remembered by the right ones.

- Don't build a megaphone. Build a platform.

- Don't chase trends. Lead them or deliberately challenge them.

- Don't broadcast. Invite dialogue.

- And above all: build authority not on volume, but on value.

Because in a distracted world, real influence doesn't come from being the loudest. It comes from being the most trusted, the most distinct, the most authentic.

Now go out there. Make your niche clear. Make your voice powerful. Build your authority without the noise.

The Burnout Rebrand: Why "Quiet Quitting" Was Just the Beginning

The New Face of Exhaustion

Burnout didn't disappear. It rebranded.

In 2022, social feeds filled with the phrase "quiet quitting." People weren't resigning from their jobs; they were rejecting the idea that endless hustle was a virtue. They started doing their jobs, no more, no less. Critics called them lazy. Economists called it disengagement. But under the surface, something deeper was happening: a generational pushback against the myth that success requires self-sacrifice.

Three years later, that rebellion has matured into something bigger. Workers aren't just refusing overtime. They're re-engineering life around sustainability. Founders are rethinking the culture they built on caffeine and crisis. Burnout has become less about being tired and more about being done. Done with toxic metrics, performative productivity, and the belief that boundaries signal weakness.

The story of burnout today isn't about quitting. It's about redefining ambition.

From Badge of Honour to Red Flag

For decades, overwork was romanticized. The first one in, the last one out - the "grindset" entrepreneur sleeping under their desk, bragging about 100-hour weeks. That image sold books and built brands. But behind the glossy founder documentaries and Instagram reels, the mental-health fallout became impossible to ignore.

A Deloitte study found that 77 percent of professionals have experienced burnout in their current job. The World Health Organization officially classified it as an occupational phenomenon. Meanwhile, productivity metrics plateaued. The irony is clear: the more we work, the less we achieve.

When Elon Musk told employees that working 80 hours a week was what "changing the world" required, younger founders rolled their eyes. They're not lazy. They just see the trade-off differently. Mental health is no longer a side conversation; it's a KPI. A founder who collapses from exhaustion isn't a hero. They're a cautionary tale.

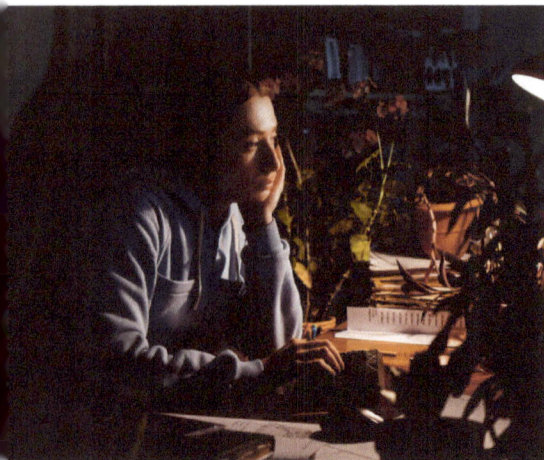

Boundaries as Strategy

The post-pandemic entrepreneur learned something powerful: boundaries don't kill momentum. They protect it. Companies that adopted four-day weeks, asynchronous communication, or flexible hours found something unexpected. Productivity didn't fall; it stabilized. Turnover dropped. Creativity spiked.

At a software firm in Austin, the CEO banned internal meetings on Fridays. It forced people to manage their own time," she

said. "Output improved by double digits, and morale soared."

This shift mirrors a larger economic reality. The knowledge economy doesn't reward endurance. It rewards clarity. You don't innovate by staring at a screen until midnight. You innovate when your brain has space to wander. Rest isn't indulgence; it's infrastructure.

That's why burnout recovery programs are giving way to burnout prevention systems - operational designs that prioritize pacing, not panic. Think mandatory recharge weeks, mental-health stipends, and asynchronous workflows that respect time zones and family life. These aren't perks. They're productivity architecture.

The Rise of the Sustainable Founder

Five years ago, the startup world worshipped speed. "Move fast and break things" was gospel. Now, entrepreneurs are re-writing it: "Move deliberately and build things that last."

Meet Lara Gómez, a serial founder who sold her first fintech startup at thirty-two. The payout was life-changing, but the aftermath was brutal. "I had money and zero health," she recalls. "I built a company that broke me."

Her second venture looks nothing like the first. No 2 a.m. Slack messages. No hero culture. Team members take quarterly sabbaticals, and deadlines flex around wellness check-ins. Growth is steady, not explosive. "It's slower," Lara admits, "but this time, I get to enjoy it."

Stories like hers are multiplying. Investors once obsessed with speed are quietly embracing longevity. Venture capital firms now track "founder sustainability scores" alongside financial metrics. The message is clear: healthy companies start with healthy leaders.

Burnout in Disguise

Burnout today doesn't always look like collapse. It hides behind phrases like "I'm just tired" or "after this launch, I'll rest." It lives in the founder who scrolls through Slack at midnight pretending they're "just checking one thing." It hides in high performers who keep functioning but stop caring.

Psychologists call this "functional burnout" when productivity survives but purpose dies. The employee still delivers, but the spark is gone. Teams that once thrived on mission drift into mechanical motion. And because the metrics still look fine, leaders miss the warning signs.

Functional burnout is dangerous because it looks like competence. The antidote is not more motivation sessions. It's honest cultural audits. Leaders must ask: Are we inspiring people or depleting them? Are we rewarding outcomes or endurance?

The Data Shift: From Hours to Health

Businesses are learning that emotional exhaustion is quantifiable. HR analytics now track burnout indicators the way finance teams track revenue. Pulse surveys measure energy, not just engagement. Tools like CultureAmp and Officevibe integrate wellbeing metrics into performance dashboards.

One multinational consultancy introduced an "energy index" that measures workload balance, recovery days, and mental-health trends across teams. Within a year, turnover dropped 18 percent. "We stopped pretending people are machines," their COO said. "We started designing like we believe it."

Meanwhile, founders are measuring themselves, too. Wearables track sleep debt. Journaling apps monitor cognitive fatigue. The data isn't just wellness fluff. It's risk management. Burnout isn't a personal failure; it's an operational cost.

Leadership After the Hustle

A new leadership archetype is emerging: **the anti-hustle leader**.

Instead of idolizing busyness, they model balance. They talk openly about therapy, digital detoxes, and saying no. They don't just grant permission for rest. They require it.

In one Fortune 500 company, executives must take a minimum of ten consecutive days offline annually. If a leader checks email, HR resets their vacation calendar. The policy was radical at first. Now, it's a bragging right. "Our leaders rest hard," the CEO told Pivot. "Because if they burn out, everyone pays."

This cultural inversion signals a broader truth: sustainable leadership is the new competitive advantage. Empathy, adaptability, and self-regulation aren't soft skills. They're survival skills.

How Work Redefined Ambition

Millennials chased titles. Gen Z chases time. That generational pivot is reshaping business design.

RSS>

Reliable Staff Solutions

STAFF SPOTLIGHT

Team Success: Sheena Spraggon

How Collaboration Creates Faster, Stronger Wins

"What I love about RSS is the teamwork, the shared ideas, and the family-like support behind every goal."

When did you join the RSS team, and what brought you here?

I joined RSS in March 2021 as a part-timer, inspired by a culture that feels less like rigid work and more like meaningful, passionate effort.

What's your favorite part of working at RSS?

At RSS, it feels like having close friends by my side. Whenever I need help or clarity, the team is always there to support me.

How has your role evolved since you started?

From part-timer to Team Manager, learning our processes helped me grow in problem-solving, communication, and leading the team.

Describe your typical workday or work-from-home setup

With good music playing, I begin by reviewing updates and ensuring smooth admin operations.

If you could describe RSS in three words, what would they be?

Synergistic, Committed, Dynamic

STAFF STATS

- 🎧 **Work Anthem:** Neo soul or light jazz playlist

- 🍪 **Favorite Snack:** Mocha coffee and potato chips

- 💡 **Fun Fact:** Drawing is my passion, and I sing too, but only in the bathroom.

"

Being reliable means showing up, following through, and staying dependable, even when it's inconvenient.

For many young professionals, ambition no longer means corporate ladders or corner offices. It means autonomy - projects that matter, freedom to travel, and energy left for life outside work. When asked what they value most, 61 percent of Gen Z respondents in a 2025 McKinsey study said "flexibility" outranked "compensation."

This shift terrifies traditional leaders who equate commitment with constant availability. But the data keeps proving them wrong. Flexibility fuels focus. Autonomy builds accountability.

When employees feel trusted to manage their time, they don't coast—they excel. Purpose is the ultimate performance enhancer.

Burnout's New Frontier: The Founder-Employee Divide

Even as companies embrace wellness, a gap remains: founders still struggle to apply those same principles to themselves. They build humane systems for teams, then quietly ignore them.

Why? Guilt. Identity. Fear. Many founders built their reputations on endurance. Slowing down feels like betrayal. But ignoring personal limits doesn't scale. It sabotages.

A leadership coach in Toronto calls it the oxygen paradox: "Founders preach balance but forget to breathe." Her clients learn to schedule recovery the way they schedule revenue meetings. "If rest isn't on the calendar," she says, "it won't happen."

Self-care for entrepreneurs isn't spa days. It's structure: delegation, digital boundaries, and honest reflection. The future of entrepreneurship depends on founders who can model sustainable ambition—not martyrdom.

Lessons from Companies That Got It Right

- **Basecamp** built its brand on calm productivity. When other startups glorified chaos, Basecamp cut hours and banned after-hours communication. Twenty years later, it's still profitable and founder-led.

- **Patagonia** institutionalized purpose over pressure. Its employees surf mid-day, take paid environmental sabbaticals, and show higher retention than most corporations triple its size.

- **Buffer**, a remote-first social-media company, publicly reports revenue, salaries, and mental-health initiatives. Transparency replaced burnout with trust.

These aren't fringe experiments. They're proof that humane systems outperform toxic ones.

What This Means for Entrepreneurs

- Treating energy as a finite resource, not an infinite one.

- Building workflows that reward focus, not presence.

- Measuring wellbeing as carefully as profit.

- Creating cultures where rest and reflection are normalised, not negotiated.

Because the truth is simple: exhaustion doesn't inspire innovation.

The rebrand of burnout marks a turning point in modern business. "Quiet quitting" was never about laziness. It was a collective act of wisdom. A refusal to keep trading life for output. The next generation of leaders isn't running from work; they're redefining what work is worth.

And that's not rebellion. That's evolution.

The Return of the Generalist: Why Versatility Is the Most Underrated Superpower

The Specialist Trap

For years, the business world worshipped specialists.

The logic seemed flawless: pick one lane, master it, and never stray. We built résumés like precision tools - tight, focused, and polished to fit a single role. Recruiters told us to niche down. Business gurus told us to "find your one thing." But somewhere between the obsession with expertise and the explosion of AI, something shifted.

The modern world no longer rewards those who know one thing deeply. It rewards those who can connect many things meaningfully.

Enter the era of the generalist. The people thriving in 2025 aren't the ones with the longest technical skill lists; they're the ones who adapt, cross disciplines, and think laterally. They're translators between worlds - part strategist, part operator, part creator. They move fluidly between industries and roles, pulling insights from everywhere.

In a world where algorithms can do the routine, the edge belongs to the flexible.

From the Age of Expertise to the Age of Adaptability

In the 20th century, industries were built on hierarchy and deep specialization. Assembly lines, corporate ladders, and fixed career paths rewarded narrow mastery. You learned one trade and stuck with it for life.

But the digital economy doesn't play by those rules. Startups scale overnight. Markets shift in a tweet. Entire industries appear and vanish within a decade. AI can write code, design ads, and analyze data in seconds, making many "specialist" tasks instantly replicable.

What remains uniquely human?

The ability to think across boundaries.

That's why the most valuable people in business today are "T-shaped" professionals: broad across disciplines, deep in one. They can see connections others miss. They can translate between departments that normally don't understand each other - marketing to engineering, data to design, finance to storytelling.

As author David Epstein wrote in Range: Why Generalists Triumph in a Specialized World, "The more complex and unpredictable the environment, the more generalists will thrive." The business landscape of 2025 fits that description perfectly.

The Myth of Mastery

We've been sold a lie: that mastery means focusing so narrowly you block everything else out. The problem is, narrow mastery struggles when the ground keeps shifting.

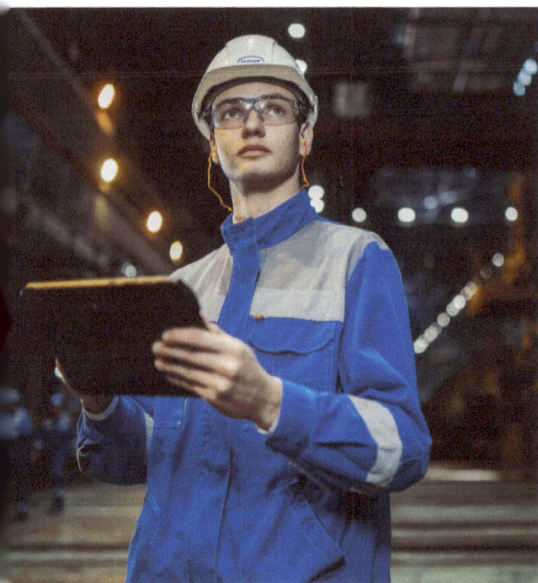

Think of Blockbuster. Kodak. Blackberry. They weren't dumb; they were specialized. Their expertise blinded them to new paradigms. Meanwhile, outsiders with broader perspectives - Netflix, Apple, and digital-first upstarts - saw the change coming.

Specialization creates comfort. Generalism creates perspective.

In a world of constant reinvention, it's not depth alone that wins. It's range.

Why Generalists Make Better Founders

Founders, especially, are rediscovering the value of versatility.

The best entrepreneurs are rarely single-lane experts. They're systems thinkers who can see the full chessboard - product, brand, finance, people, culture - all at once. They may not be the best at each individually, but they understand how everything interacts.

Elon Musk can discuss rocket propulsion one minute and social media algorithms the next. Sara Blakely went from selling fax machines to inventing shapewear to building a billion-dollar brand with humor and storytelling. Richard Branson started with records, then airlines, then telecoms, all while understanding people more than any particular industry.

Being a generalist doesn't mean knowing everything. It means knowing how things relate.

And in leadership, that's priceless.

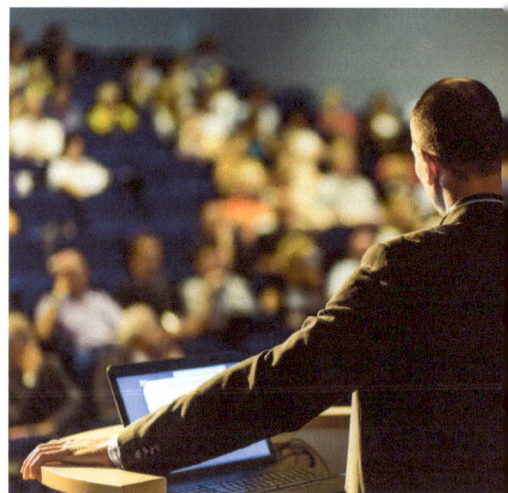

The Hybrid Professional

The modern workforce is dominated by hybrids - people who defy job titles.

A marketer who codes. A designer who writes. A lawyer who builds AI workflows.

Hybrid talent is what powers innovation. A McKinsey report found that teams composed of "integrators"—employees with overlapping skill sets—produce up to 35% higher innovation output than siloed teams. Why? Because creativity thrives in intersections.

A hybrid team doesn't get stuck in jargon wars. They translate. They connect dots. They build bridges between isolated expertise.

That's also why startups and small businesses are disproportionately innovative. They can't afford pure specialists for every role. They hire curious doers who wear multiple hats and that constraint becomes their creative advantage.

The Power of Curiosity

Generalists are powered by curiosity - the compulsion to explore beyond their comfort zone. That curiosity is what makes them resilient in volatile markets.

When AI tools emerged, specialists panicked. Copywriters feared extinction. Designers feared replacement. But the generalists, the ones curious enough to learn the tools and reimagine their work, thrived. They didn't see AI as a threat; they saw it as leverage. Curiosity turns uncertainty into opportunity. It's the mindset shift that defines this new era of work.

As one founder said in a Pivot interview: "I don't hire for experience anymore. I hire for curiosity. Skills get outdated. Curiosity doesn't."

The Career Arc Is Dead

The linear career, climb one ladder, retire at the top, is over.

Today's professionals are building career portfolios, not career paths.

A portfolio career is a blend of roles, industries, and side projects that evolve over time. It's how people hedge against volatility and stay intellectually alive. A marketing director might freelance in UX design. A finance

consultant might teach online. A startup founder might invest in local coffee shops.

This isn't distraction, it's diversification.

It also reflects a broader psychological shift: identity isn't tied to one profession anymore. People want to explore multiple callings. And in doing so, they bring cross-pollinated wisdom wherever they go.

The most resilient leaders are those who treat their careers like ecosystems, not assembly lines.

What Businesses Gain from Generalists

Organizations built entirely on specialists often look efficient on paper but rigid in practice. They struggle to pivot when markets change.

That's why forward-thinking companies are rebalancing their hiring strategies. They're creating "generalist lanes", roles designed for people who can float between functions, experiment across projects, and connect teams.

Google famously encourages employees to spend 20 percent of their time on projects outside their job description. That policy birthed Gmail and Google News.

IDEO, the design firm behind Apple's early products, hires "T-shaped" thinkers deliberately. Their internal motto: "We hire curiosity, not credentials."

The result? A culture that thrives on exploration instead of compliance.

Why The Generalist Is the Future of Leadership

Tomorrow's leaders won't be the ones who know every detail of a spreadsheet. They'll be the ones who know how to bring the right people together to solve problems that don't even exist yet.

Leadership used to mean authority. Now it means orchestration.

The generalist leader doesn't micromanage; they synthesize. They can walk into a room of specialists - data scientists, creatives, financiers and extract the one insight that unites them all. They make complexity coherent.

That's why multidisciplinary thinking is being woven into leadership programs at top business schools.

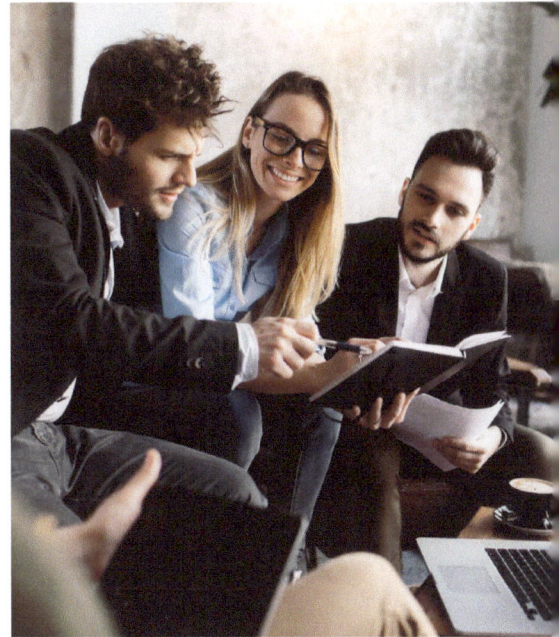

Harvard's "Systems Leadership" track and Stanford's "Interdisciplinary Thinking Labs" are teaching executives to think like connectors, not controllers.

When the pace of change outstrips your ability to plan, your only advantage is adaptability.

The Renaissance Is Digital

The term "Renaissance person" feels romantic, but it's suddenly relevant again. The original Renaissance was about fusing art, science, and philosophy into progress. Today's version fuses tech, creativity, and empathy.

The digital renaissance is being led by people who defy categories - engineers who make art, educators who build apps, influencers who teach economics through storytelling.

The internet made knowledge free. AI made execution faster. The next edge is synthesis - turning scattered information into coherent innovation.

Being a generalist isn't nostalgic; it's revolutionary.

How to Cultivate Range

For professionals or founders who've spent years in one lane, becoming a generalist doesn't mean abandoning expertise. It means broadening context.

1. Cross-train intentionally.

Learn one skill outside your comfort zone every quarter - coding if you're a marketer, finance if you're creative, psychology if you're in management. Range compounds.

2. Collaborate with opposites.

Innovation happens at intersections. Pair engineers with artists, strategists with analysts. Build mixed teams that challenge each other's assumptions.

3. Tell better stories.

Generalists often excel as communicators because they can translate complexity. Whether pitching investors or leading teams, storytelling is the bridge between expertise and action.

4. Embrace seasonality.

There will be seasons of deep focus and seasons of exploration. Both matter. The goal isn't balance, it's rhythm.

5. Redefine success.

Success for a generalist isn't about being "the best" at one thing. It's about being indispensable across many.

What This Means for Entrepreneurs

If you're building a business in 2025, hire for curiosity, not just credentials. Look for pattern-thinkers who can bridge silos, not just execute tasks. Encourage side projects, rotation programs, and shared ownership.

If you're a founder, give yourself permission to evolve. You don't have to be the same kind of leader you were when you started. Your business will demand different versions of you as it grows.

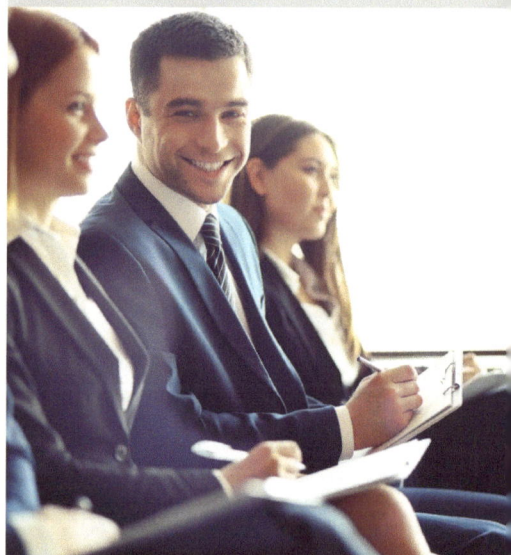

And if you're an individual navigating your career, remember this: depth still matters, but breadth keeps you alive.

Because in a world that changes by the month, the only real expertise is adaptability.

The generalist is back. And this time, they're not unfocused, they're unstoppable.

The Founder's Dilemma: Growth vs. Freedom

When Growth Stops Feeling Like Success

There comes a point in every founder's journey when growth, the very thing you once chased, starts to feel like a trap.

At first, it's intoxicating. The sales charts go up. Investors start calling. You hire fast, build a team, expand into new markets, and watch your brand name spread. But then comes the shift. Suddenly you're managing managers, not building products. Your calendar fills with back-to-back meetings instead of big ideas. And the company that once gave you freedom now feels like a machine you serve.

This is the founder's dilemma, when the pursuit of growth collides with the desire for control, meaning, and quality of life.

The world taught us that success means scaling. But in 2025, more entrepreneurs are asking: At what cost?

The Myth That More Is Better

For decades, startup culture glorified scale as the ultimate proof of success. "If you're not growing, you're dying," became gospel. Investors pushed for faster rounds, bigger valuations, and global expansion.

But growth without alignment doesn't liberate founders. It consumes them.

The deeper truth is that not every business is meant to become a unicorn. Some are meant to be thoroughbreds, built for endurance, not explosion.

Take the software company Basecamp. While competitors chased VC funding, Basecamp stayed small by design. Founders Jason Fried and David Heinemeier Hansson deliberately capped headcount and rejected acquisition offers. They chose profit over hype, autonomy over ego. The result? Two decades of sustainable success, zero burnout, and total creative control.

Their philosophy is simple: "Work

doesn't have to suck to succeed."

The New Definition of Growth

Founders in 2025 are rewriting what it means to grow. Growth is no longer purely financial—it's philosophical. It's about depth, not just width.

- Depth of impact: Building something that genuinely improves lives.

- Depth of mastery: Getting better at your craft rather than just expanding operations.

- Depth of autonomy: Structuring your business so you can actually live the life you built it for.

Growth that compromises freedom isn't growth, it's drift.

Consider Aliyah Torres, founder of a design studio that scaled from a freelance operation to a 40-person agency in three years. The numbers looked good. But she was miserable. "I built the company I thought I was supposed to build," she admits. "Then I realized I didn't even want to run an agency. I wanted to create."

Last year, she restructured her business, downsizing to 12 employees and focusing on high-value creative strategy. Revenue dipped slightly. Profit soared. Her schedule cleared. "For the first time in years," she says, "I feel like a founder again."

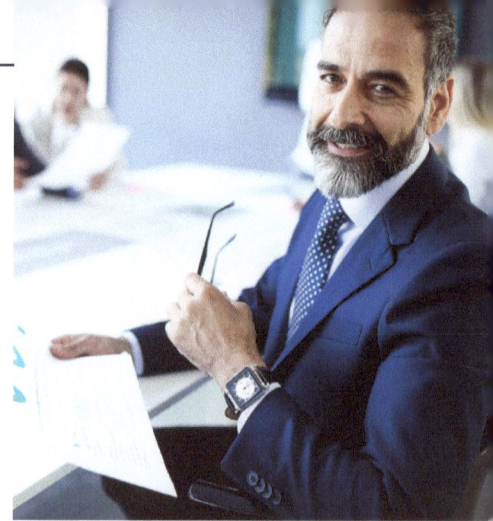

Freedom Metrics: The New KPIs

In this new era of entrepreneurship, founders are tracking different metrics, what we can call **Freedom KPIs**.

- **Autonomy Index:** How much of your time do you control each week?

- **Purpose Alignment:** How often does your work feel meaningful?

- **Stress Ratio:** How often do you feel calm vs. reactive?

- **Profit per Hour:** How much value are you creating relative to your effort?

These aren't vanity numbers. They're sustainability indicators.

Imagine if founders reviewed their freedom metrics with the same seriousness they give to P&L sheets. It would change the entire game. Because a business that costs you your peace of mind isn't a business. It's a cage with branding.

When Investors Want Speed but You Want Space

The founder-investor relationship often becomes a tug of war between purpose and pressure.

Investors crave velocity. They're rewarded for exits, not endurance. Founders crave flexibility. They're rewarded for staying alive. Somewhere between those goals lies friction.

That's why more entrepreneurs are choosing to grow without traditional funding. Bootstrapping, once seen as a constraint, has become a strategy. It forces clarity, discipline, and customer-centric thinking. It keeps ownership intact and timelines sane.

Take ConvertKit, the email platform for creators. Founder Nathan Barry turned down multiple acquisition offers and raised minimal outside capital. His reasoning? "I didn't start this to serve investors. I started it to serve creators and that includes me."

By growing slower, ConvertKit built stronger. It crossed $40M in annual recurring revenue with full founder control.

Growth without freedom is unsustainable. But freedom without direction is chaos. The trick is balance, growing just enough to amplify your impact, but not so much that you lose yourself.

The Psychology of Enough

Every founder reaches the question eventually: What's enough?

Enough revenue to live comfortably. Enough reach to make an impact. Enough scale to sustain a team but not so much that it devours your life.

The problem is, "enough" is a moving target. Success creates appetite. You hit one milestone and instantly raise the bar.

Psychologists call this the hedonic treadmill. The tendency to keep chasing satisfaction that never sticks. It's what drives founders to keep expanding even after they've "made it."

But there's power in defining your ceiling early. Some call it a "Freedom Cap"—the point at which growth shifts from liberating to limiting. Knowing that number can save founders years of unnecessary stress.

Freedom, after all, isn't just financial. It's emotional, creative, and temporal. It's being able to take a walk in the middle of the day because you built something that runs without you.

The Rise of Lifestyle Empires

The phrase "lifestyle business" used to sound small. Dismissive. But that stigma is dying fast.

Today, founders are building lifestyle empires - high-profit, low-complexity businesses that serve both purpose and personal freedom. They don't chase scale. They chase systems.

Think of creators who build six- or seven-figure ecosystems around niche audiences. Fitness coaches with digital courses, e-commerce owners with automated logistics, consultants who sell intellectual property instead of hours.

They're not smaller, they're smarter.

They've learned that scalability isn't just about headcount or funding. It's about leverage.

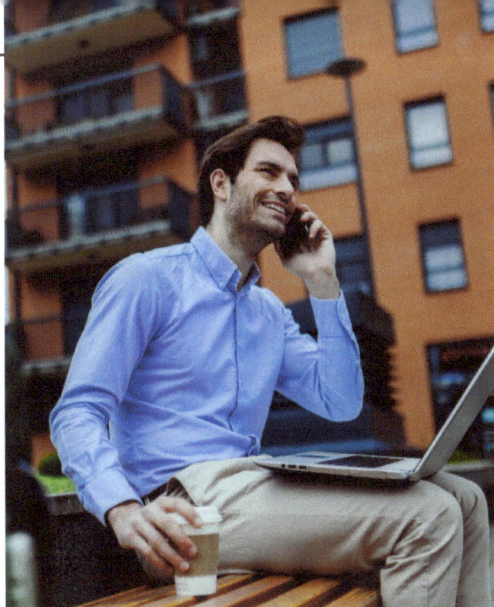

Automating the repetitive, outsourcing the unnecessary, and doubling down on what energizes you.

Freedom doesn't mean doing less. It means doing what matters more often.

When Growth Becomes Identity

Here's the hard truth: some founders cling to growth because it's tied to their identity.

When your self-worth is built on momentum, slowing down feels like failure. That's why burnout so often masquerades as ambition. The founder says they're "just pushing for one more quarter" when really, they're scared of stillness.

Stillness forces reflection. And reflection often reveals uncomfortable truths, like the fact that your business no longer fits who you've become.

Entrepreneurship isn't static. The founder who started your company isn't the same person running it five years later. If your company doesn't evolve with you, it will eventually suffocate you.

Sometimes, the bravest move isn't scaling up. It's scaling back.

Case Studies in Conscious Growth

1. Patagonia: Founder Yvon Chouinard famously gave away his company, not to investors, but to the planet. By transferring ownership to a trust that ensures profits go toward climate action, he redefined what "exit" means. His legacy isn't expansion. It's alignment.

2. Wildbit: Before it was acquired, Wildbit operated for

years as a calm company - profitable, remote, and purpose-driven. Founders Chris and Natalie Nagele ran it on 32-hour weeks with full salaries. Their secret? A simple mantra: "We work to live, not live to work."

3. Nomad Capitalist: Built on the idea of global freedom, founder Andrew Henderson scaled deliberately, not recklessly. His team is small, his margins high, and his travel schedule flexible. It's empire design with lifestyle at the center.

These stories share one theme: growth can serve freedom, but only if freedom stays the goal.

Designing a Business That Doesn't Own You

To build sustainably, founders must flip a few old assumptions:

1. Growth isn't linear. There will be seasons of acceleration and seasons of stabilization. Both are productive. The pause is where vision refines.

2. Profit beats perception. Revenue makes headlines. Profit makes freedom. Focus on margins and efficiency before chasing volume.

3. Systems equal sanity. Automate decision-making where possible. Create SOPs not to bureaucratize, but to buy back mental bandwidth.

4. Clarity is your compass. Revisit your "why" every year. If your strategy no longer matches your values, adjust. The business should serve you, not define you.

5. Redefine winning. Winning might look like a smaller team, a slower pace, or a shorter week. That doesn't make it less ambitious. It makes it sustainable.

What This Means for Entrepreneurs

The founder's dilemma is no longer a warning. It's a rite of passage.

Every entrepreneur who builds something meaningful will eventually face it. The question isn't whether to grow; it's how much growth you can live with.

The next era of entrepreneurship won't be dominated by those who scale fastest. It'll be led by those who scale consciously.

Freedom is the ultimate KPI. It's not about escaping work; it's about designing work that lets you stay human.

So ask yourself: if your business doubled tomorrow, would your life improve or implode?

The answer to that question will tell you everything about whether you're building success or just building walls around yourself.

Because the real flex in 2025 isn't growth.

It's control.

Beyond the Algorithm: Building a Brand That Doesn't Depend on Social Media

When the Feed Turns Against You

For years, the mantra was simple: post more, grow faster. The path to brand visibility seemed paved by algorithms - likes, shares, and followers. But in 2025, that path feels more like a treadmill. Every update from Meta, TikTok, or X rewrites the rules. Engagement drops overnight. Ads cost more, reach less, and the platforms that once empowered small businesses are now squeezing them dry.

For many founders, social media has shifted from opportunity to obligation. They're spending more time feeding the machine than building their businesses. And the question echoing across boardrooms and Slack channels is simple: *What happens if the algorithm stops liking you?*

The answer is driving one of the biggest strategic pivots in modern entrepreneurship. The rise of **off-platform brands**.

The smartest companies aren't abandoning social media.

They're outgrowing it.

The Illusion of Reach

The average organic reach for a business account on Instagram hovers below 5 percent. On Facebook, it's often closer to 2. If your brand has 10,000 followers, only a few hundred actually see your content.

Meanwhile, AI-generated noise floods the feed. Everyone is publishing more, but attention isn't expanding, it's fragmenting. Algorithms reward controversy, not credibility. The result is a digital paradox: more content, less connection.

Brands are realizing that virality doesn't equal loyalty. A viral video may deliver dopamine, but rarely delivers dollars. Sustainable growth comes from depth, not breadth, from relationships, not reach.

That's why the savviest entrepreneurs are shifting from "social media strategy" to community ecosystem design.

The Return to Owned Audiences

The term "owned audience" is back in vogue and for good reason.

An owned audience is one you can reach directly without permission from a third-party platform. It's your email list, your SMS subscribers, your membership portal, your podcast listeners. It's the digital version of owning your land instead of renting it.

In 2025, owned channels are outperforming social in engagement, conversion, and longevity. Open rates on well-targeted newsletters hover around 40 percent—eight times higher than typical Instagram engagement.

Look at Morning Brew. The media company started as a daily newsletter for business students. Today, it reaches millions and has spun off podcasts, events, and community products. All powered by email, not algorithms.

Or consider Notion. The productivity platform built its empire on content that lives in searchable hubs and learning communities, not fleeting social feeds.

When you own your distribution, no algorithm update can silence you.

Building a Direct Relationship Economy

The algorithm-free brand operates like a local coffee shop with a global footprint. It knows its regulars by name.

Instead of chasing impressions, these brands build interactions. They invite dialogue, not drive-by engagement. They host online workshops, closed Slack groups, member portals, and private events. They turn customers into collaborators.

A fitness entrepreneur might replace her Instagram challenge with a private coaching group on Circle. A skincare brand might shift from influencer campaigns to direct education through a Substack newsletter.

These aren't just new tactics, they're new philosophies.

Social media turns customers into metrics. Direct ecosystems turn them into communities.

The Algorithm Dependency Problem

When platforms control your visibility, they also control your narrative. Brands start shaping content to please algorithms instead of serving audiences. Creativity flattens into trends. Authenticity gives way to optimization.

Worse, dependency distorts decision-making. Teams spend more time tracking analytics dashboards than tracking customer satisfaction. Marketing becomes reactionary.

And the most dangerous illusion of all: thinking that a large following equals a loyal base.

A founder with 100,000 followers but no direct contact list is one platform policy away from obscurity. But a founder with 5,000 email subscribers and a clear message can sustain a business indefinitely.

The Power of Slow Content

Off-platform brands are embracing slow content - work that lasts longer than a 24-hour cycle.

Think articles, podcasts, guides, and digital products that live in evergreen hubs. These assets compound value over time instead of expiring overnight.

SEO, once overshadowed by social media buzz, is enjoying a renaissance. Google's focus on "experience and authenticity" is rewarding deep, original content again. Thought leadership blogs, resource libraries, and how-to videos are drawing audiences tired of surface-level posts.

One SaaS founder put it bluntly: "I stopped posting every day and started publishing once a week but with depth. My traffic doubled, and I stopped feeling like a hamster."

Slow content doesn't mean boring. It means strategic permanence.

From Audience to Community

The biggest shift in brand building is from broadcast to belonging.

Audiences watch. Communities participate.

When you stop chasing visibility and start cultivating belonging, everything changes. Your followers become advocates. Your marketing becomes mutual. Your customers start defending your brand before you do.

A great example is Duolingo. The app's community forums, streak-based gamification, and local events turn language learners into a movement. The brand's social presence amplifies that energy. It doesn't create it.

Community-driven companies grow slower at first, but they grow deeper. And in 2025's volatile economy, depth is resilience.

Diversifying Digital Real Estate

Smart founders treat digital presence like an investment portfolio - diversified, balanced, and future-proof.

They combine three layers of digital real estate:

1. Rented Space (social platforms) - Great for discovery, storytelling, and awareness. But never the home base.

2. Owned Space (websites, email, apps) - The foundation. These channels gather leads, host content, and build data independence.

3. Earned Space (PR, partnerships, collaborations) - The amplifier. When other people talk about you, it drives credibility and traffic to your owned assets.

The ideal mix looks less like a funnel and more like an ecosystem, each piece feeding the next.

This layered approach ensures that if one channel falters, the others sustain momentum.

The Email Renaissance

Ironically, one of the oldest tools in digital marketing is having its biggest comeback.

Email isn't sexy, but it's stable. It's algorithm-proof, personal, and measurable. It lets brands communicate like humans, not broadcasters.

Modern newsletters blend editorial storytelling with commerce. Brands like Beardbrand, Glossier, and TinySeed use newsletters not just to sell, but to think aloud to share lessons, behind-the-scenes stories, and ideas that create intimacy.

Email is where attention slows down long enough for trust to grow. And in a marketplace addicted to speed, that slowness is an advantage.

Brands That Broke the Algorithm Habit

- **Patagonia** built its brand around environmental activism, not advertising. Its email and documentary storytelling drive loyalty deeper than any feed ever could.

- **Ben Francis's Gymshark** began as a social phenomenon but transitioned to a hybrid ecosystem, podcasts, events, and membership apps, to avoid overreliance on social reach.

- **MrBeast**, one of YouTube's biggest creators, diversified his empire with burgers, chocolate bars, and philanthropic ventures - each with its own customer database and media engine.

The pattern is clear: the more successful the brand, the less it depends on any single platform.

The Algorithm Isn't the Enemy; It's Just Not the Strategy

Social media still matters because it's the place where discovery happens. It's often the first touchpoint where audiences stumble across your ideas, your message, or your brand. But discovery isn't destiny, and it shouldn't be the finish line.

The smartest brands treat social platforms as entry points, not endpoints. Every post has a job: guide people toward a deeper connection. That might mean an email signup, a resource hub, a private community, or a product experience where real engagement can grow. When you build these next steps intentionally, you stop fearing the algorithm because your success no longer depends on it. You're not chasing likes; you're creating momentum that moves people closer to meaningful action.

Brands that understand this shift treat social media as a stage, a place to perform, spark interest, and invite people in. But they never confuse the stage with the whole show.

What This Means for Entrepreneurs

If your business depends entirely on the whims of social media, you don't own your audience, you're borrowing it.

The next era of brand growth will belong to those who:

- Build ecosystems, not funnels.

- Prioritize depth of relationship over reach of message.

- Create evergreen content that compounds, not posts that evaporate.

- Treat email, community, and education as the true engines of connection.

It's tempting to chase the next viral trend. But real influence isn't measured in followers. It's measured in who shows up when the algorithm doesn't.

In the end, the brands that survive aren't the loudest.

They're the ones that own their voice.

Money with a Mission: The Rise of Conscious Capitalism in a Divided Economy

The Shift from Profit to Purpose

For over a century, capitalism has been defined by one word - growth. Bigger markets, bigger profits, bigger everything. But in a world fractured by inequality, climate change, and distrust, a growing number of business leaders are asking a radical question: *What if capitalism could serve more than shareholders?*

Welcome to the age of conscious capitalism where purpose isn't a slogan but a system. Where the bottom line includes not only profit, but people and the planet.

It's a movement reshaping boardrooms, startups, and consumer expectations. From B-Corps to benefit corporations, from regenerative supply chains to transparent pay, business is evolving from extraction to contribution.

And while critics dismiss it as marketing gloss, the numbers tell another story. Purpose-driven companies outperform their peers by 42 percent in long-term growth and employee retention. Consumers are voting with their wallets. Investors are following the money.

Purpose, it turns out, has a profit model.

Capitalism at a Crossroads

The cracks in the old system are impossible to ignore. Rising costs, widening wealth gaps, and social unrest have made "business as usual" feel out of touch.

Younger generations, raised on

transparency and activism, are demanding something different. They don't want brands that take a stand. They want brands that stand for something.

A 2025 Edelman Trust Barometer survey revealed that 78 percent of consumers believe companies have a moral responsibility to address social issues, even when it comes with short-term costs. That level of expectation is reshaping how modern businesses operate.

Leaders can no longer rely on quarterly reports or financial performance alone to earn trust. Every purchasing decision, hiring choice, partnership, and supply chain link is being examined through a values-driven lens. Consumers want to see alignment between what a company says and what it actually does.

The age of neutral business is over, replaced by a landscape where accountability is the baseline.

From CSR to DNA

Corporate Social Responsibility used to sit in its own department. Today, it operates as a design principle woven into the foundation of the business. The old CSR playbook, donating a small portion of profits and calling it impact, is fading fast. The modern model builds responsibility into the heart of operations, shaping how brands develop products, choose partners, and communicate with customers.

Consider Allbirds, the sustainable footwear company. Its mission to create better things in a better way influences everything from the materials it sources to its carbon labeling on every product. Customers aren't simply buying shoes; they're supporting a philosophy that aligns with their values.

Then there's Tony's Chocolonely, a Dutch chocolate brand dedicated to ending slavery in cocoa production. They publish

open-source reports, expose systemic issues, and pay farmers higher premiums to ensure ethical sourcing. Their radical transparency created a loyal global following.

Brands like these prove that doing good isn't an afterthought or a marketing angle. It's a strategic advantage. Integrating purpose into the core of the business doesn't just inspire

trust. It differentiates, attracts modern consumers, and builds long-term market power.

The Investor Evolution

For years, socially responsible investing was a niche hobby. Today, it's mainstream capital. ESG (Environmental, Social, and Governance) funds surpassed $40 trillion globally in 2024, and even traditional investors are rethinking metrics.

Larry Fink, CEO of BlackRock, said it best: "Climate risk is investment risk." But beyond climate, there's cultural risk - brands that ignore ethics now face reputational collapse overnight.

The modern investor doesn't just ask, What's the return? They ask, What's the impact?

Platforms like SeedInvest and Republic allow retail investors to fund mission-based startups directly. Meanwhile, family offices and venture funds are launching "impact tranches," tying founder bonuses to measurable sustainability outcomes.

Profit no longer excuses harm. It proves stewardship.

The Consumer Revolution

Every purchase is now a referendum.

Shoppers are not just comparing

prices, they're comparing principles. They scan QR codes to see carbon footprints, boycott brands tied to exploitation, and share receipts of companies that give back.

Gen Z, in particular, treats spending as activism. A 2025 Nielsen report found that 73 percent of Gen Z consumers will pay more for ethical products. They aren't naive, they're strategic. They know capitalism isn't disappearing, so they're reshaping it from the inside out.

This cultural awareness has given rise to the "conscious consumer stack", a set of values buyers check before checkout:

- **Sustainability:** Does it harm or heal the planet?

- **Equity:** Who benefits and who's left behind?

- **Transparency:** What's the brand hiding or revealing?

The brands that answer these questions with honesty earn loyalty that money can't buy.

Conscious Doesn't Mean Cute

Let's be clear: conscious capitalism isn't kumbaya. It's not soft, sentimental, or idealistic. It's disciplined strategy. It's ruthless efficiency disguised as empathy. Reducing waste trims operational costs. Treating employees well lowers turnover, which preserves institutional knowledge and avoids constant rehiring expenses. Ethical sourcing strengthens long-term supply stability, cutting the volatility that comes with questionable partners. Diversity broadens perspectives, fuels innovation, and improves decision-making at every level.

Look at Unilever. When the company pledged to cut its environmental footprint in half, critics insisted it would sacrifice profit. The opposite happened. Its Sustainable Living brands became the company's top performers, growing 69 percent faster than the rest of the portfolio. Customers rewarded

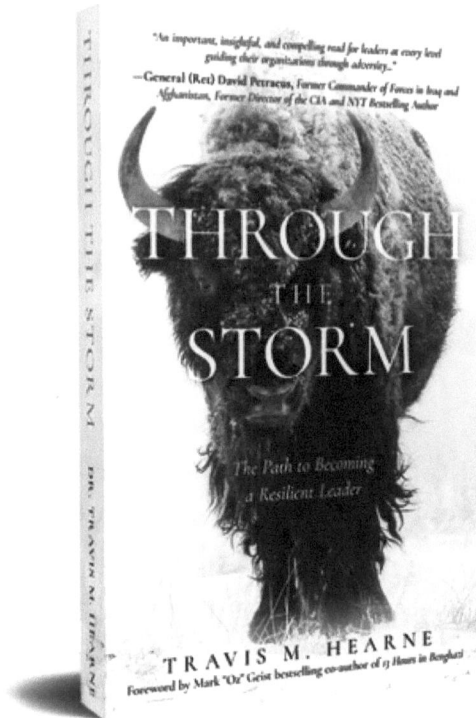

the commitment, not the caution.

Or consider Patagonia, which famously launched its "Don't Buy This Jacket" campaign. Instead of hurting revenue, the campaign boosted sales by 30 percent. Why? Because honesty builds credibility, and credibility drives loyalty. People buy from brands they trust, especially in a crowded marketplace where authenticity is often missing.

Doing good isn't charity, it's strategy. It builds resilience, sharpens competitive advantage, and creates compounding returns that money alone can't buy. Trust compounds faster than capital, and businesses that understand this win in the long run.

The Founder's Awakening

A new breed of entrepreneur is leading this charge: founders who see profit and purpose not as opposites, but as partners.

They're pragmatic idealists - builders who understand that capitalism is a tool, not a villain.

Consider Yvon Chouinard, who transferred ownership of Patagonia to a trust ensuring all profits fight climate change. Or Whitney Wolfe Herd of Bumble, who built a billion-dollar company around female empowerment and safety.

Closer to home, micro-founders are embedding mission at the seed stage: eco-packaging startups, ethical fintechs, and inclusive fashion brands that prioritize transparency from day one.

They're proving that impact isn't the reward for success, it's the reason for it.

The Cultural Backlash

Not everyone is convinced by the rise of conscious capitalism. Critics dismiss it as virtue-washing - PR glossed with sustainability buzzwords. They

argue that a system built on profit can never truly be conscious. And to be fair, some companies reinforce that skepticism. A green label here, a diversity slogan there, or a polished ESG report often hides practices that are anything but ethical. These brands adopt the language without doing the work.

But the market is becoming harder to fool. Digital watchdogs like Good On You, Ethical Consumer, and other ratings platforms publicly grade companies on their real-world impact. Social media exposes contradictions in hours, not months. Consumers no longer wait for annual reports. They investigate, share screenshots, and mobilize communities instantly. Transparency isn't a nice-to-have anymore. It's survival.

In a way, the backlash is necessary. It applies pressure, sharpens standards, and forces companies to walk their talk. It keeps the movement honest by pushing businesses to back claims with action.

Conscious capitalism isn't about being flawless. It's about being accountable, evolving, and choosing better practices even when they're harder. Progress, not perfection, is the point.

Redefining the Bottom Line

Modern companies are moving beyond a single metric of success. Instead of focusing purely on profit, many are adopting the "triple bottom line," a framework that evaluates impact on three pillars: Profit, People, and Planet. Profit ensures the business stays financially healthy. People reflect how responsibly the company treats employees, customers, and communities. Planet measures the organisation's environmental footprint and long-term sustainability practices.

But an increasing number of companies are adding a fourth dimension: Purpose. Purpose is the deeper reason the business exists, the north star that connects actions to meaning. It turns strategy into story, giving employees something to believe in and customers a mission they can participate in. Without that "why," even strong ethical efforts risk feeling like surface-level compliance rather than genuine commitment.

Purpose creates emotional gravity. It attracts the right talent, strengthens loyalty, and shapes decisions that reach far beyond quarterly results. Simon Sinek's insight captures it well: people don't buy what a company does. They buy why it does it. Conscious capitalism is simply that idea scaled across an entire organization, anchoring performance in principles that matter.

Small Business, Big Impact

You don't need to be Patagonia to practice purpose.

A local café that pays fair wages, sources locally, and offers community space is a conscious business. A solopreneur who builds educational products that empower others is, too.

The key isn't scale, it's intention. Small businesses can actually move faster. They can make transparent decisions, test sustainable packaging, or introduce profit-sharing models without bureaucracy. They lead by example, showing that purpose scales down as easily as it scales up.

And in communities fractured by distrust, these micro-leaders often have the most authentic impact.

Designing for Regeneration

The next evolution of conscious capitalism goes beyond sustainability to regeneration, leaving systems better than you found them.

Regenerative agriculture. Circular manufacturing. Restorative hiring that uplifts marginalized talent.

Businesses are no longer asking how to minimize harm. They're asking how to reverse it.

Imagine a fashion label that grows its own materials or a construction firm that rebuilds ecosystems as it develops land. These aren't hypotheticals. They're emerging case studies across Europe and Southeast Asia.

Regeneration reframes capitalism not as extraction, but as renewal.

What This Means for Entrepreneurs

Founders entering 2025 face a choice: chase short-term profit or build long-term purpose. The first creates revenue; the second creates relevance.

To join the movement without falling into the virtue trap:

- **Start with values, not marketing.** Mission statements should drive operations, not decorate websites.

- **Measure impact like profit.** Track social and environmental ROI with the same rigor as financial returns.

- **Be transparent when you fail.** Authenticity builds more trust than perfection.

- **Design for contribution.** Ask, "What does my business give back to the ecosystem that sustains it?"

Because in a divided economy, neutrality is the riskiest position of all.

Conscious capitalism isn't about rejecting profit. It's about redefining what profit stands for.

The future belongs to those who prove that doing well and doing good are the same act performed at different scales.

Money with a mission isn't a trend.

It's the blueprint for the next chapter of capitalism itself.

The Trust Deficit: Why Transparency Is the Real Competitive Advantage

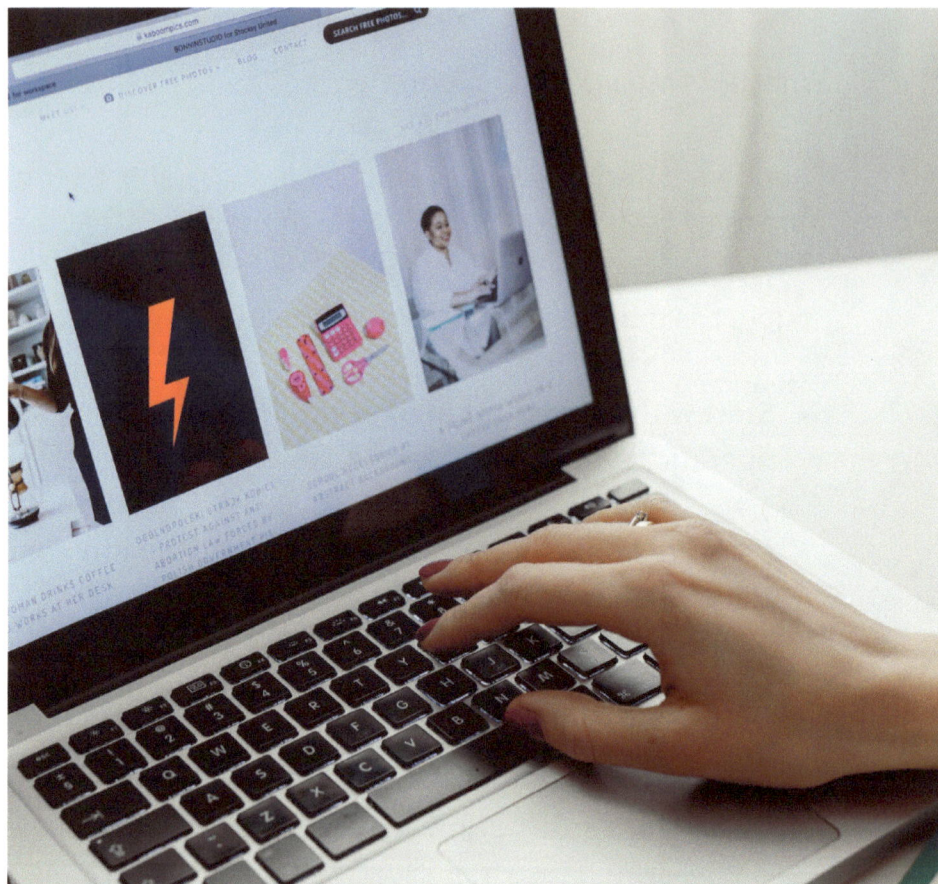

The Age of Skepticism

Trust used to be assumed. You bought from a brand because it said what it did and did what it said. But somewhere along the digital highway, that trust broke down. Fake reviews, deepfakes, inflated ESG claims, and AI-generated everything have created an economy of suspicion.

In 2025, the biggest problem facing businesses isn't competition, it's credibility. Consumers don't just want good products; they want proof.

A Pew Research survey this year found that 68 percent of Americans believe corporations "intentionally mislead" the public in advertising. Among Gen Z, that number jumps to 82 percent. The more polished your brand looks, the more skeptical they become.

We live in a post-trust economy. And that's exactly why transparency is emerging as the ultimate differentiator.

When Authenticity Became Strategy

In the early days of social media, brands were told to "be authentic." But authenticity was treated as a tactic - share a few behind-the-scenes photos, use a casual tone, maybe show your CEO wearing sneakers.

Then the world got smarter.

Consumers learned to see through "relatable" marketing. They started fact-checking in real time. They realized most "transparency" was performance.

Real authenticity isn't an aesthetic, it's accountability. It's not what you say about your values; it's how you prove them when no one's watching.

That's why the next evolution of branding isn't storytelling, it's story showing.

The Collapse of Institutional Trust

The erosion of trust isn't limited to marketing, it's systemic. Governments, banks, media outlets, and even nonprofits have all suffered credibility crises.

Business, ironically, is one of the few institutions still seen as capable of leadership. The Edelman Trust Barometer shows that people now trust "my employer" more than traditional media or political systems.

That puts enormous responsibility, and opportunity, on today's leaders.

When institutions fail, the companies that step into that vacuum with integrity win loyalty that lasts decades.

Think of Patagonia's decision to give away its profits to the planet. Or Airbnb's transparency in the wake of the pandemic when it refunded millions in bookings and opened homes to refugees. These moments aren't marketing, they're moral signals.

Trust is the new brand equity.

Radical Transparency: The Next Business Model

Radical transparency doesn't mean oversharing every decision. It means removing the invisible walls between your company and your community.

It means:

- Publishing pricing structures openly.

- Sharing supply chain data.

- Being honest about margins, emissions, and mistakes.

- Releasing diversity stats without PR spin.

When brands own their imperfections, they earn credibility.

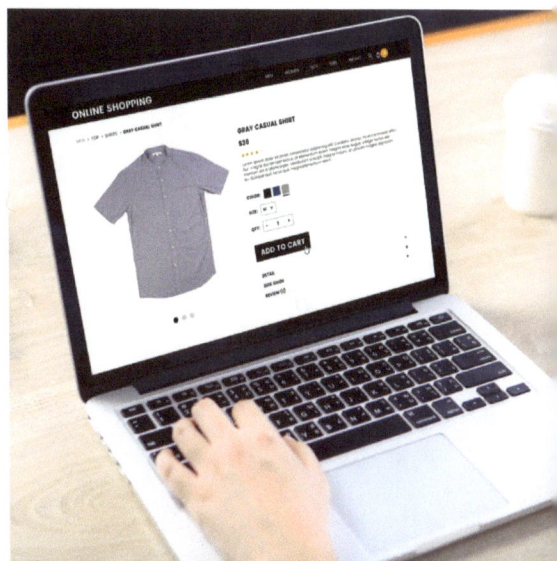

A clothing startup in Copenhagen called *ASKET* posts the full cost breakdown of every item on its website - materials, labor, transport, markup. Customers know exactly what they're paying for, and sales continue to rise.

Transparency doesn't scare buyers, it empowers them.

The Algorithm Made Us Liars

Digital marketing, for all its precision, trained businesses to manipulate. SEO tricks, clickbait headlines, "limited time offers" that never end. The entire online ecosystem was built to hack attention.

The side effect? Exhausted audiences.

Every exaggerated promise chips

JOIN
Achieve Systems

BECOME AN ACHIEVE SYSTEMS MEMBER TODAY!

Education
We help you get the tools to create a thriving business! It's turnkey, you can start NOW!

Marketing
We provide marketing guidelines but also plug you into our conferences, events and database

Community
We have a thriving community of entrepreneurs and business owners for you to collaborate, refer and partner with to grow and up-level your business!

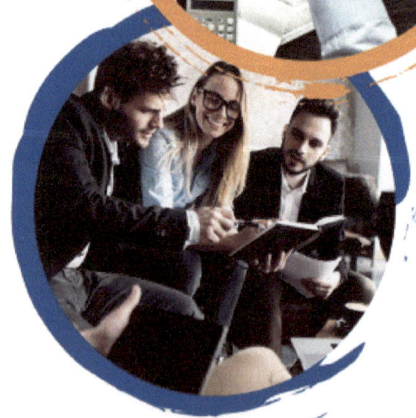

WE WORK WITH ENTREPRENEURS, BUSINESS OWNERS, SPEAKERS & LEADERS!

CONTACT US OR REGISTER HERE: www.AchieveSystemsPro.com

away at credibility. Every overproduced ad erodes emotional connection. Consumers are tuning out noise in favor of clarity.

The winners of 2025 aren't the loudest brands. They're the most honest ones.

The companies thriving in this era have one thing in common: they tell the truth even when it hurts.

The Transparency Flywheel

Here's the paradox: transparency feels risky, but it compounds trust faster than any ad campaign.

When companies disclose information willingly, they reduce speculation. Speculation breeds distrust. Openness breeds ownership.

That dynamic creates a "trust flywheel":

- **Honesty builds confidence.** Customers stop second-guessing motives.

- **Confidence drives loyalty.** Repeat buyers increase lifetime value.

- **Loyalty drives advocacy.** Customers become marketers.

- **Advocacy attracts new buyers.** Credibility scales organically.

Each turn of the flywheel strengthens the brand, reinforcing the connection between what the company promises and what it delivers. Over time, these consistent actions compound, creating a

reputation that becomes harder for competitors to imitate. When trust becomes the primary moat, rivals can copy products or messaging, but they can't duplicate the credibility earned through sustained alignment and reliability.

The Cost of Secrecy

Secrecy used to be seen as sophistication. Apple built mystique around product launches, and luxury brands thrived on exclusivity. But what once symbolized prestige now signals opacity.

When businesses hide too much, consumers assume the worst.

The past few years have seen companies implode under the weight of withheld truths:

- Theranos collapsed because secrecy masked fraud.

- FTX unraveled when opaque accounting was exposed.

- Boeing faced public outrage after internal communications revealed hidden safety issues.

The lesson is clear: opacity is expensive. Transparency may sting short term, but it saves your brand long term.

Transparent Leadership

Transparency isn't just an external strategy. It's an internal culture standard. Employees are customers of the company's leadership, and they expect the same clarity and honesty that consumers demand. They want to understand pay structures, growth paths, expectations, and the overall direction of the organization. When leaders hide behind closed doors or communicate in vague, infrequent updates, morale erodes and trust fades.

Research from MIT Sloan shows the impact clearly: companies with strong, transparent communication see 30 percent higher employee engagement and 23 percent lower turnover. In a hybrid, post-pandemic work environment, overcommunication has become a core leadership skill. Silence breeds anxiety; clarity builds stability and confidence.

This is why many modern CEOs choose to share weekly internal memos, open access to financial dashboards, and even publish summaries of board meetings for their entire team. When employees understand the "why" behind decisions, not just the "what", they feel included, empowered, and aligned. Teams rally behind the mission rather than guessing at the mystery.

Blockchain, once hyped for crypto, is now powering traceability in supply chains. Consumers can scan QR codes to verify product origins, worker wages, and sustainability data.

Platforms like Provenance and Everledger are helping brands authenticate materials in industries from fashion to diamonds.

AI, ironically, may help restore trust too, when used to verify instead of fabricate. Tools that detect AI-generated content, trace image origins, and flag false data are becoming standard.

The Transparency-Tech Alliance

Technology is catching up to transparency.

The future of marketing won't belong to the best storytellers but to the brands that can back their claims with proof.

Transparency as Culture, Not Campaign

Too many brands still treat transparency as a seasonal marketing push - something to spotlight when convenient. But trust doesn't switch on and off. It's a habit.

That habit starts with leadership. Transparent cultures invite accountability at every level. They empower teams to speak up, share challenges, and solve problems before they explode.

Buffer, the social media company, built its entire brand on radical transparency: open salaries, published revenue dashboards, and honest retrospectives. The result? Fierce loyalty from both employees and customers.

Transparency creates alignment. Everyone knows what game they're playing and why it matters.

The New ROI: Return on Integrity

In a crowded marketplace where everyone is competing for attention, integrity has become something you can measure, not just a feel-good value. Brands with strong trust ratings consistently outperform those that rely on clever messaging alone. Forrester Research found that companies leading their category in trust see 1.6x higher purchase intent and twice the level of customer advocacy. That kind of loyalty can't be manufactured. It comes from alignment between what a brand claims and how it behaves.

Trust also lowers acquisition costs because belief replaces persuasion. Customers who trust you don't need hard selling, they move with confidence. Over time, they become ambassadors who extend your reach far beyond your own marketing efforts.

Integrity isn't just a virtue anymore. It's a measurable growth strategy that carries real financial weight, shaping everything from customer lifetime value to market positioning. Brands that commit to it earn more than attention. They earn loyalty.

What Transparent Brands Look Like in 2025

- **They publish mistakes.** When something goes wrong, they address it publicly before anyone asks.

- **They talk like humans.** No corporate jargon. Just clarity.

- **They educate, not just advertise.** They teach audiences about process, impact, and value.

- **They listen visibly.** Feedback isn't hidden. It's displayed, discussed, and acted on.

- **They invite collaboration.** Communities help shape products, policies, and priorities.

Transparency isn't about perfection, it's about participation.

What This Means for Entrepreneurs

For founders and leaders, transparency is no longer optional. It's the oxygen of modern business.

To thrive in a skeptical world:

- Build trust before traction. Credibility scales faster than clicks.

- Replace mystery with metrics. Show, don't spin.

- Share process, not just polish. People believe what they can see.

- Make honesty your brand asset. It's the one thing competitors can't copy.

Trust, once broken, takes years to rebuild, but once earned, it compounds forever.

The next generation of iconic companies won't win by out-advertising others. They'll win by out-trusting them.

Because in a world drowning in information, truth is the rarest currency left.

AI and the New Credibility Crisis: Who Do We Trust When Everyone Sounds the Same?

The Machines Learned to Talk And We Forgot How to Listen

In 2025, anyone can sound smart. Anyone can publish a "thought leadership" post. Anyone can generate a 20-page whitepaper in minutes. And that's exactly the problem.

AI didn't just democratize content creation. It flooded the world with sameness. Scroll through LinkedIn, Instagram, or even news websites, and you'll start to notice it. Content that feels polished but hollow. Emails that read clean but generic. Blog posts with structure but no soul.

It's not that humans suddenly got dull. It's that AI made it easy to manufacture competence.

And when everyone sounds competent, no one feels credible.

The result? A global credibility crisis.

People don't know who to trust - brands, influencers, institutions, even experts. The line between authentic insight and auto-generated filler has blurred, and consumers are responding with the one defense they have left: **skepticism**.

AI didn't break trust by existing.

We broke trust by outsourcing authenticity.

The Death of the "Expert Voice"

For decades, expertise was signaled by tone. The academic tone. The consultant tone. The "I know what I'm talking about" tone. But generative AI learned those tones frighteningly well.

Suddenly, expertise wasn't a skill, it was a prompt.

MICROCASTING

Supercharge Your Business!

Do you want to find new ways to add additional income to your coaching, consulting, or content creation business?

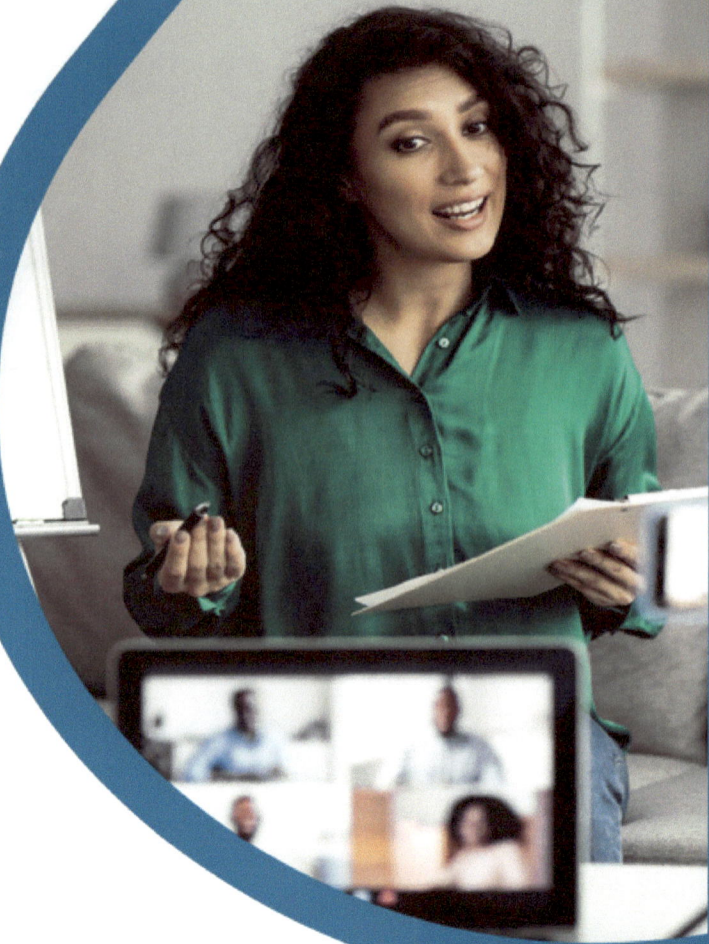

eLearning Portals by Microcasting is specifically designed for Coaches, Consultants, and Course Creators to engage your customers, establish yourself as a thought leader, and grow your revenues.

Here are just a few things you can do with **Microcasting**:

- ⊘ **Start selling** your courses and programs.
- ⊘ Create a **paid membership site** to grow your revenues.
- ⊘ Build a free membership site to **increase lead gen**.
- ⊘ Easily **integrate eLearning** into your marketing website.
- ⊘ Create **individualized customer portals** .
- ⊘ And so much more...

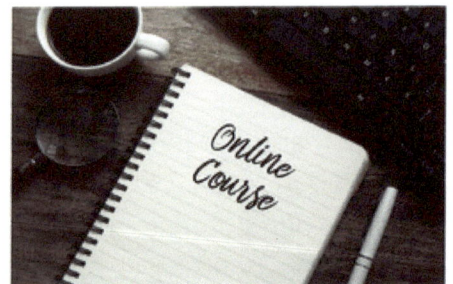

Microcasting is an all-in-one online learning platform that makes it easy for course creators to design, manage, and market their courses. With its personalized eLearning experience, you can keep your current customers engaged with your business, generating more upsells and higher renewal rates. Create courses quickly and effortlessly - all with the help of Microcasting!

Try Microcasting today and start transforming your business!

Request a demo - email us at ✉ info@microcasting.com **OR VISIT** ⊕ www.elearning-portals.com

In minutes, AI can write:

- a convincing legal summary

- a market analysis

- a product review

- a technical explanation

- a journalistic article

So convincingly that even trained eyes get fooled.

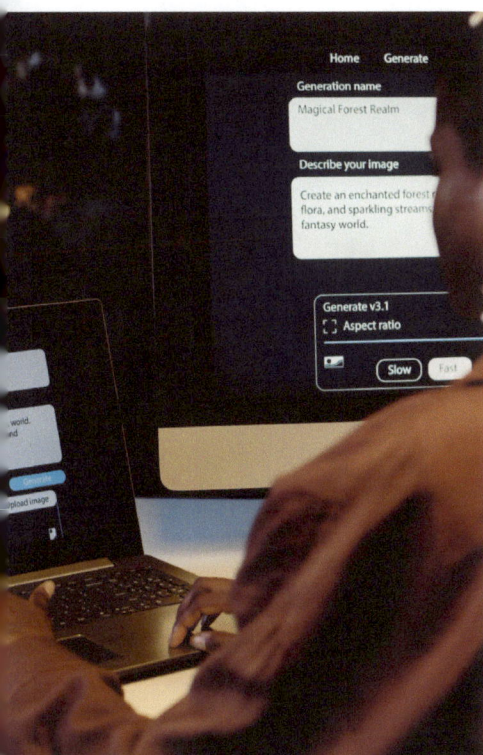

We never learned to distinguish authority from articulation.

We trusted polished writing and formal language as indicators of intelligence. Now that machines can mimic both, the entire credibility hierarchy is collapsing.

The question isn't "Can you express ideas clearly?"

And that changes everything.

When Authenticity Becomes the Last Differentiator

We're entering a strange paradox:

The more AI content fills the world, the more valuable human voice becomes.

Consumers are gravitating toward content that feels raw, imperfect, and emotionally charged because messy is the new credible.

The rise of "imperfect content" is everywhere:

- Podcasts with unedited tangents

- YouTube videos with awkward pauses

- Influencers admitting mistakes

- CEOs showing behind-the-scenes

- Brands posting unscripted moments

What used to look unprofessional now looks trustworthy.

AI is optimized for precision.

Humans are optimized for resonance.

And in a credibility crisis,

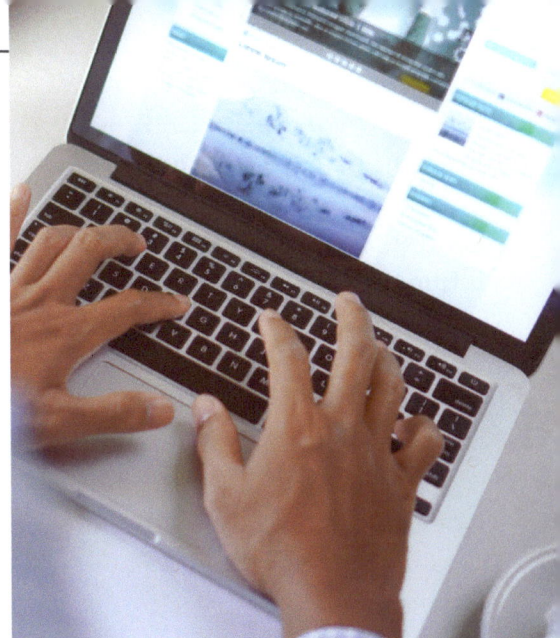

resonance wins.

The Signal Problem: Noise vs Meaning

The internet used to reward creators who posted the most. AI changed that equation. Now anyone can post the most, effortlessly.

A single person can publish:

- 100 tweets

- 5 blogs

- 20 carousel posts

- 3 sales emails

- 1 e-book

all before lunch.

The result: digital noise at unprecedented scale.

And in noise, meaning gets lost.

Consumers feel overwhelmed, not informed. Businesses feel pressured, not empowered.

Leaders feel invisible, not influential.

This is why credibility is becoming the most valuable resource in the digital economy.

Not content. Not visibility.

Credibility
.
Only the trusted will be heard.

The Rise of the "Verified Human" Economy

As AI-generated content explodes, new technologies are emerging to verify authenticity:

- **Digital watermarking** - Tools like C2PA mark whether content is AI-generated.

- **Proof-of-humanity protocols** Blockchain systems that confirm content came from a verified human source.

- **AI detection tools -** Imperfect but improving.

- **Reputation-based verification -** Platforms ranking creators by historical accuracy and transparency.

Human credibility is becoming quantifiable.

Think of it as the new version of the blue check mark but actually earned.

Brands Are Being Forced to Pick a Side

The era of "We use AI" is ending.

The new era?

"Here's where we don't."

Brands are leaning into human-first positioning as a differentiator:

- Restaurants advertising "No AI in our recipes"

- Fashion brands showcasing human designers

- Consultants emphasizing manual research

- Journalists pledging "human-written" stories

- Companies adding transparency tags to content

Consumers aren't anti-AI, they're anti-deception.

The brands that admit where they use AI (and where they don't) will earn trust.

Those that fake it will collapse.

Because authenticity is not just a marketing angle anymore.

It's a risk management strategy.

The New Credibility Drivers

If content polish no longer signals expertise, what does?

1. Lived Experience

People want insight rooted in real

stories, not synthesized summaries.

2. Transparency

Showing the process behind the message is now more persuasive than the message itself.

3. Contrarian Thinking

AI is trained on patterns. Humans break them.

4. Granular Detail

AI generalizes. Humans recall specifics. ("The café on 9th that used to serve curry bread before it burned down" beats "a café I used to visit.")

5. Emotion

AI mimics emotion but doesn't generate it. Humans do.

6. Real-Time Reaction

AI responds quickly, but not contextually in the way humans do.

Live discussions, messy debates, spontaneous reactions, that's where human credibility shines.

Thought Leadership Is Evolving, Fast

Before AI, thought leadership meant being polished, articulate, and consistent. Now? Thought leadership requires proof-of-thought, not proof-of-writing.

Tomorrow's thought leaders won't win by publishing frequently, AI already does that.

They'll win by thinking differently.

The leaders emerging right now are:

- Philosophical
- Analytical
- Transparent
- Vulnerable
- Experiential
- Community-driven

In short: undeniable humans.

Thought leadership is shifting from "Here are my insights" to **"Here's how I arrived at them."**

Process is becoming more persuasive than prose.

Creators Are Adapting in Unexpected Ways

The credibility crisis is sparking new creative trends:

Long-form comeback

In-depth articles, essays, and videos feel harder for AI to fake.

Unedited formats

Live streams, raw audio, and casual conversations feel more trustworthy.

Niche segmentation

Creators are specializing in micro-topics AI can't easily replicate.

Human signatures

Creators are adding personal markers - verbal tics, hand-written notes, voice idiosyncrasies, to signal authenticity.

The irony?

To build credibility, creators must be more human than ever before.

AI took over the content factory.

Humans took back the creative frontier.

The Ethical Crisis Inside Companies

Behind closed doors, companies are panicking. Many built content strategies entirely dependent on AI. Some got caught publishing fake expert opinions. Others accidentally used AI-generated images in official reports.

The lesson?

AI isn't dangerous.

Unregulated AI workflows are.

Companies now need internal guardrails:

- Clear AI-use policies

- Disclosure standards

- Internal verification teams

- Crisis protocols

Because one AI slip can destroy a decade of trust.

In a world where deepfakes can fabricate CEOs, brands must proactively reassure their audiences:

"This is real. This is verified. This is us."

The Trust Recession Is Real But Fixable

The credibility crisis feels unsettling, but it's also the catalyst for a massive shift:

People are craving truth more than ever.

Trust is scarce.

Scarcity creates value.

Value creates opportunity.

Brands that lead with integrity will dominate the next decade.

We're witnessing a return to:

- relationship-based business

- human-first leadership

- community-driven loyalty

- reputation over reach

- thoughtfulness over volume

This isn't just a technological shift.

It's a cultural correction.

What This Means for Entrepreneurs in 2025

If everyone sounds the same, your competitive advantage isn't what you produce. **It's how real you are.**

To stay credible in an AI-saturated world:

1. **Show your work**. Bring people behind the curtain.

2. **Build a recognizable voice.** Distinctiveness beats polish.

3. **Use AI, but don't hide it.** Transparency is trust.

4. **Share lived experience.** AI doesn't have memories.

5. **Value depth over frequency.** Meaning beats consistency.

6. **Create in public.** Human process > artificial perfection.

7. **Build community, not just content.** Trust lives in relationships, not algorithms.

Because the future won't belong to those who post the most.

It will belong to those who are trusted the most.

And in an era where anyone can generate content, trust is the only thing AI will never replicate.

Work Without Borders: How Global Collaboration Is Redefining What a Team Looks Like

The New Workforce Isn't Local. It Isn't Even National. It's Planetary.

In 2025, the idea of a "local team" sounds almost quaint.

The new office isn't a building, it's a borderless network.

Your marketing lead might be in Manila. Your developer could be in Lagos. Your operations coordinator might work nights in Dublin. Your executive assistant could dial in from Bogotá or Bangkok.

The pandemic didn't just normalize remote work. It accelerated a global rebalancing of talent. For the first time in history, businesses can hire the best person for the job, not the closest. Work has become the world's most powerful passport.

Welcome to work without borders. A seismic shift that is transforming companies, cultures, and the very definition of leadership.

This isn't outsourcing.

This is **global collaboration**, and it's rewriting the rules of business.

The End of the Local Monopoly

Before 2020, proximity dictated opportunity. You worked for companies in your city. You climbed corporate ladders built on zip codes. You competed with people who lived within a 30-mile radius.

Those days are gone.

Remote infrastructure made talent borderless, and suddenly a founder in Chicago can hire a designer in Nairobi who outperforms local candidates at half the cost, not because of exploitation, but because global wage standards vary enormously.

This shift isn't flattening the playing field, it's expanding it.

For talent, it means access.

For companies, it means choice.

For economies, it means redistribution.

A developer in Vietnam can earn a Silicon Valley salary.

A small business in Scotland can afford enterprise-level support by hiring globally.

A startup in Toronto can scale using a hybrid team without burning through capital.

Talent is no longer local currency.

It's global capital.

The Rise of the Global Micro-Team

The traditional structure of business looked like this:

Build a local office. Hire full-time employees. Scale by adding more people in the same place.

Today?

Companies scale through distributed micro-teams, small pockets of high-performance talent assembled across continents.

A typical global micro-team may include:

- A founder or strategist

- A global operations specialist

- A project manager in a different timezone

- Freelance or fractional experts

- A flexible workforce of remote contractors

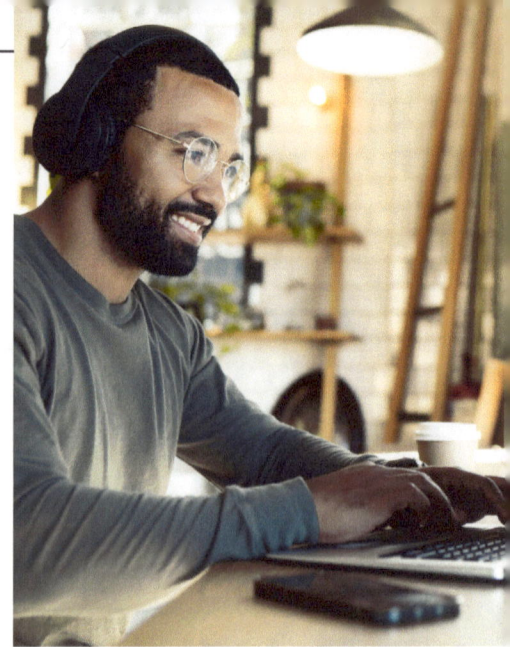

This structure isn't chaotic.

It's efficient.

You get 24-hour business coverage because time zones stack productivity.

You get diverse thinking.

You get cultural fluency.

You get resilience - one city's blackout doesn't take down the whole company.

Companies that adopt micro-teams don't just scale faster, they scale smarter.

Why Borders Became Irrelevant

There are five major forces behind the global-collaboration boom:

1. High-speed connectivity everywhere

Affordable access transformed remote work from a luxury to a standard.

2. Collaboration tools matured

Slack. Notion. Asana. Zoom. Loom. ClickUp. Remote-first isn't a workaround, it's a workflow.

3. Talent shortages in developed countries

Companies in the US, UK, and Europe simply can't fill roles fast enough locally.

4. Economic volatility

Global labor diversification reduces risk and cost.

5. Rising skill markets in emerging economies

Countries like the Philippines, Nigeria, Kenya, India, Colombia, Brazil, and Vietnam have exploding pools of skilled professionals with world-class training.

Borders didn't just dissolve, they became irrelevant.

The Cultural Intelligence Advantage

A borderless team isn't just a cost advantage, it's a strategic advantage.

Multicultural teams outperform homogeneous ones dramatically in:

- innovation

- problem-solving

- customer empathy

- marketing resonance

Why?

Because global teams see the world more completely.

A US team can't fully understand Asian buying psychology.

A European marketing team won't instinctively nail Latin American communication styles.

A North American sales team won't naturally grasp cultural formality in the Middle East.

But a team built from everywhere sees everything.

This is cultural intelligence as a competitive weapon.

The companies winning in 2025 are the ones treating diversity not as a compliance metric but as a performance engine.

The New Leadership Challenge: Managing Time Zones

Leading a global team requires new leadership muscles.

The old model of "everyone online from 9 to 5" doesn't apply when your team spans 12 time zones.

Leaders must learn how to:

- create asynchronous workflows

- reduce dependency on real-time meetings

- communicate in writing clearly

- build workflows that don't require constant check-ins

- document everything so no one is blocked

The best global teams aren't run by micromanagers.

They're run by architects - leaders who design systems, not schedules.

Asynchronous teams thrive on clarity, not control.

The Freelance-Class Revolution

Remote work didn't just globalize hiring, it globalized entrepreneurship.

Millions of professionals worldwide are now building "solo enterprises":

- specialized freelancers

- virtual assistants

- fractional executives

- remote consultants

- micro-agency owners

These individuals operate like small businesses, often serving clients in multiple countries simultaneously.

The world has quietly shifted from "employee vs employer" to "partner vs partner."

Work is evolving into global cross-collaboration rather than strict hierarchy.

This shift is liberating workers and giving businesses unprecedented flexibility.

The Ethical Divide: Fairness vs Exploitation

A global labor market introduces ethical complexity.

Some companies use global hiring to exploit cheap labor.

Others use it to uplift global communities and pay above-local standard wages.

The brands thriving long-term are the ones choosing fairness.

Ethical global teams pay competitive local rates, offer stability, and invest in professional development. They create opportunity, not extraction.

Treating global workers like true partners, not outsourced labor, is the difference between sustainable collaboration and silent resentment.

Conscious global hiring isn't charity.

It's good business.

Loyalty grows where respect lives.

The New Global Office: Platforms That Run the World

Entire industries are emerging to support borderless work:

- Gusto Global handles international payroll.

- Deel simplifies compliance in 150+ countries.

- Remote.com acts as an Employer of Record.

- Wise and Payoneer move money across borders instantly.

- Loom replaces 80% of meetings.

- Notion and ClickUp serve as universal HQs.

Your "office" isn't a building.

It's a software stack.

And the stack is the culture.

The Human Side of Global Collaboration

Borderless teams aren't transactional, they're deeply human.

Because global work does something profound:

It increases empathy.

When you work with people across cultures, you learn to slow down, listen more, ask questions, and communicate with intention. You learn patience. You learn perspective.

A founder in Kansas learns how to collaborate with a designer in Pakistan.

A marketer in Cape Town learns

how to co-create with a strategist in Melbourne.

A remote assistant in the Philippines becomes the operational backbone of a company in Canada.

These connections reshape worldviews.

Global teams don't just build businesses, they build bridges.

The Myth of In-Person Superiority

There's a stubborn belief that in-person teams outperform remote ones.

But research continues to prove the opposite.

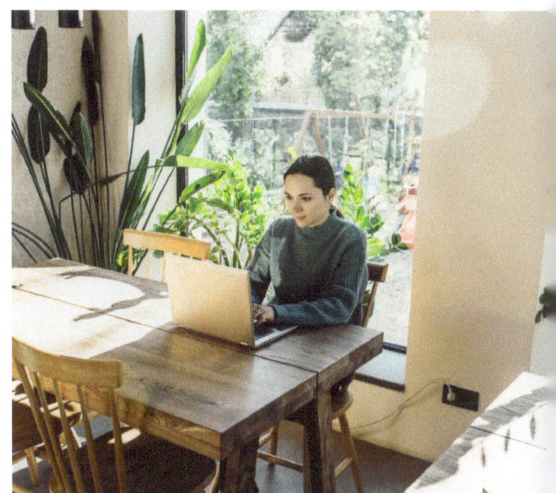

Stanford economist Nick Bloom's studies reveal:

- Remote teams are 13% more productive

- Turnover is significantly lower

FOR EVERY BUSINESS & BUDGET

Looking for a website design firm or D.I.Y. platform that can help you build a visually stunning and effective online brand? Look no further than our expert team. At Proshark, we help you build a customized website that meets your unique needs and goals and converts visitors to customers.

PROSHARK SITES

INNOVATION DESIGNED TO INSPIRE

www.proshark.com

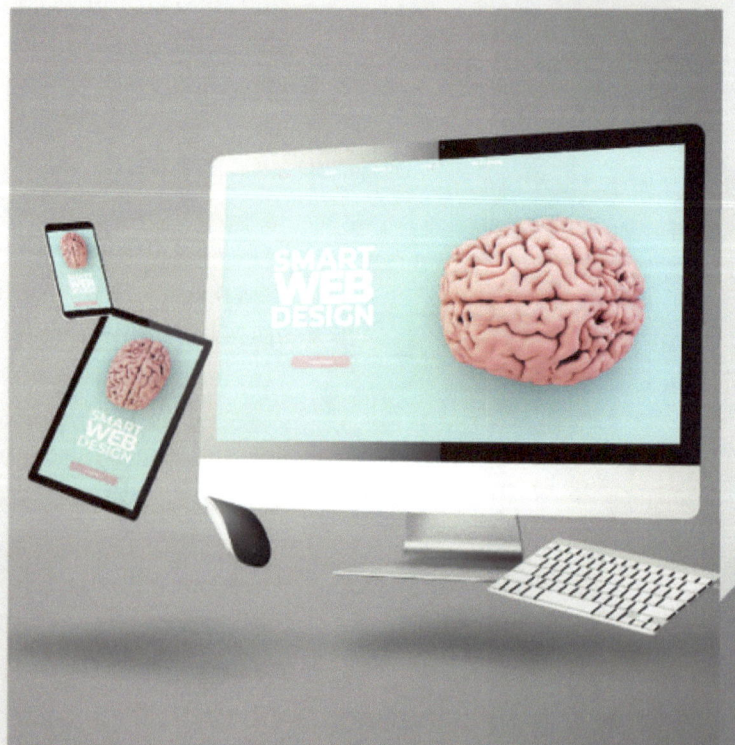

- Focus is higher

- Work-life satisfaction skyrockets

In-person isn't better.

It's just familiar.

The companies insisting on office-first strategies aren't optimizing productivity, They're feeding nostalgia.

Meanwhile, remote-first companies build *results-first* cultures.

No one cares where you work.

They care whether the work works.

Global Hiring as a Superpower for Small Businesses

Large corporations were early adopters of global talent.

Now small businesses are catching up and often doing it better.

A local business with a small budget can hire:

- a world-class graphic designer

- a seasoned operations manager

- a brilliant copywriter

- a skilled virtual assistant

...all without breaking the bank.

Global talent isn't just accessible, it's transformational.

Small businesses with big dreams finally have the team to match.

The Hidden Benefit: 24-Hour Productivity

Borderless work creates time-zone stacking, a 24-hour workflow without burnout.

Here's how it looks:

- Team A works while Team B sleeps

- Team B picks up where Team A left off

- Projects move twice as fast

- No one works overtime

- Deadlines collapse

- Execution accelerates

This isn't hustle culture.

It's handover culture.

It's the future of operational efficiency.

The Future Team: Flexible, Fluid, and Free

The companies that survive the next decade won't have rigid structures.

They'll have fluid networks of talent that adapt to market needs.

Teams will expand or contract like elastic.

People will contribute across multiple companies at once.

Work will look more like collaboration than employment.

The idea of "one job, one company, one office" will feel ancient by 2030.

We're entering the age of decentralized workforces where the best work comes from anywhere.

Borders aren't barriers anymore.

They're irrelevant.

What This Means for Entrepreneurs

If you're building a company today, your biggest advantage isn't funding or connections, it's talent.

And talent is everywhere.

To thrive in a borderless world:

- Hire for skill, not geography.

- Build asynchronous workflows.

- Document everything.

- Establish cultural norms intentionally.

- Invest in global team relationships.

- Adopt ethical pay practices.

- Use tech as your HQ, not a crutch.

The next iconic companies will be built by teams that never meet in person yet collaborate like family.

Work without borders isn't the future.

It's the present.

And the founders who embrace it now will lead the next revolution of business.

The Great Unfollow: When Consumers Start Walking Away from Influencer Culture

Influence Isn't Dying, It's Evolving.

The influencer economy once felt unstoppable. Millions followed strangers on the internet as if they were trusted friends. Brands poured billions into sponsored content. Everyday people became celebrities overnight. The formula seemed simple: build a following, sell a lifestyle, cash out.

But something shifted.

The likes still exist. The views still rack up. The campaigns still run. But the trust? The trust has evaporated.

In 2025, consumers aren't just unfollowing accounts.

They're unfollowing entire ecosystems of staged authenticity, curated perfection, and algorithm-optimized personas.

This isn't the death of influence.

It's the collapse of artificial credibility.

Welcome to **The Great Unfollow**, the moment when audiences stopped believing the internet and started demanding proof that people are real.

The Era of Overexposure

There was a time when influencers felt aspirational.

Their curated feeds provided a glimpse into lives that looked perfect but possible. But saturation killed the magic.

Their curated feeds provided a glimpse into lives that looked perfect but possible. But saturation killed the magic.

We passed the point of too much.

Too much selling.

Too much sameness.
Too much manufactured vulnerability.
Too much "relatable" content that... wasn't.

When every influencer uses the same presets, reads the same scripts, and promotes the same products, the illusion cracks.

Audiences began asking:

Do these people believe anything they post?

And when the answer was unclear, they unfollowed.

The Authenticity Backlash

The major shift came when authenticity stopped feeling authentic.

Influencers began announcing mental health breaks with staged crying selfies.

They posted "unedited" photos that were clearly edited.

They shared "transparent" stories crafted by PR teams.

They promoted products they admitted they never used.

The result?

Consumers felt manipulated, not inspired.

A 2025 Nielsen study found that 61 percent of Gen Z actively distrust influencer recommendations, and only 12 percent believe influencers are "genuine." That used to be the foundation of the industry.

This mistrust wasn't sudden, it was cumulative.

One over-polished apology.

One too-obvious sponsorship.

One too-perfect vacation.

Authenticity became parody.

And audiences opted out.

The Rise of the Anti-Influencer

The algorithm didn't collapse.

The trust did.

But something fascinating replaced traditional influencers: the anti-influencer.

These creators don't try to be perfect.

They don't curate aesthetics.

They don't perform relatability.

They document reality.

Messy kitchens.

Unflattering lighting.

No-makeup honesty.

Real struggles, not manufactured ones.

Their content doesn't look good but it feels true.

"De-influencing," once a fringe

trend, exploded into a mainstream movement. Creators began telling their audiences what not to buy, exposing overpriced brands, debunking viral fads, and rejecting sponsored deals that didn't align with their values.

A trust economy rose from the ashes of a hype economy.

This shift didn't kill influence, it reset the rules.

When Influence Became a Full-Time Job

Influencing stopped being fun the moment it became a job with KPIs.

Creators were pressured to:

- post daily
- optimize thumbnails
- track engagement

- chase trends
- monetize every hobby
- never take breaks

The algorithm rewarded predictability, not humanity.

And audiences noticed the burnout.

Creators who once shared slices of life became content factories, churning out posts engineered to hit metrics rather than express meaning.

The soul left the content.

The audience left soon after.

Influencers didn't fail.

The model did.

Consumers Want Meaning, Not Marketing

Today's consumer behavior looks radically different:

- They prefer recommendations from

micro-communities, not macro-celebrities.

- They trust small creators more than big ones.
- They follow people who share values, not aesthetics.
- They reward education, not persuasion.
- They crave honesty, not aspiration.

People aren't unfollowing humans.

They're unfollowing performance.

The age of polished influence is ending.

The age of real influence is beginning.

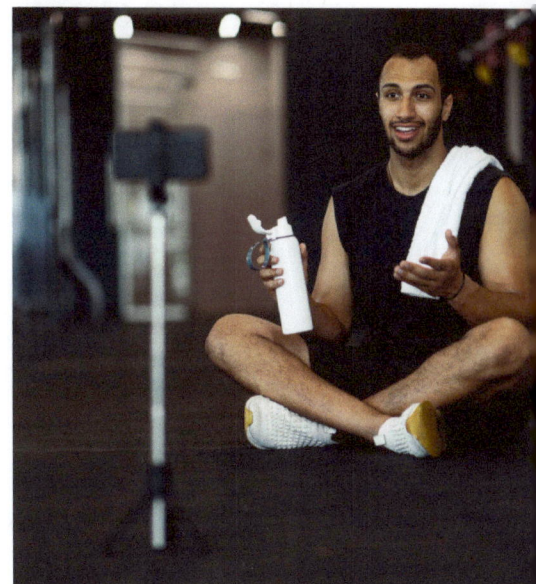

The Shift Toward Niche Credibility

Influence is no longer about reach, it's about relevance.

Creators with 2,000 deeply aligned followers outperform those with 200,000 passive ones because niche communities create real trust.

Consumers now ask:

Does this person actually know what they're talking about?

The new influencers are experts, not entertainers:

Creators were pressured to:

- the dietician debunking wellness myths

- the mechanic giving honest car-buying advice

- the former HR manager teaching salary negotiation

- the science educator breaking down misinformation

Expertise is trending again.

Competence is trending again.

Honesty is trending again.

The Great Unfollow didn't end influence, it filtered it.

The Creator-Consumer Contract Is Being Rewritten

The old contract:

"I make content, you buy what I promote."

The new contract:

"I create value, you support my work."

This shift explains why creators are building ecosystems instead of feeds:

- paid communities

- newsletters

- digital courses

- private podcasts

- behind-the-scenes memberships

- direct brand collaboration without middlemen

Platforms like Substack, Patreon, Kajabi, and Circle enable creators to build sustainable digital businesses without depending on reach-driven algorithms.

The result?

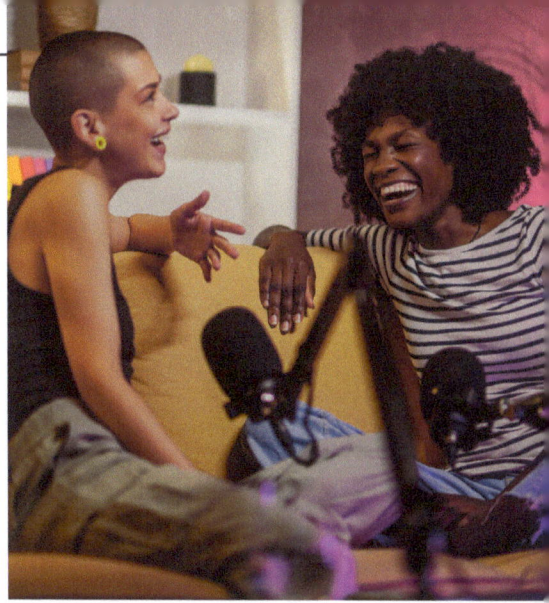

Less pressure.

More depth.

Real relationships.

Creators are rediscovering creativity.

Consumers are rediscovering trust.

Brands Are Scrambling to Adapt

Influencer marketing isn't dying but brands must evolve.

Now audiences want the moments in between, the ones that reveal something real.

The highlight reel is losing cultural power because everyone knows it's curated.

The blooper reel is gaining power because it's human.

The most viral content of 2025?

- failed cooking videos
- honest day-in-the-life clips
- budgeting breakdowns
- real-time reactions
- unfiltered opinions
- vulnerable storytelling

Perfection is no longer influential.

Imperfection is.

Old Approach

Pay for reach.

Pay for aesthetics.

Pay for followers.

New Approach

Pay for alignment.

Pay for lived experience.

Pay for credibility.

Brands now prioritize:

- creators who use their products
- transparent long-term partnerships
- content that feels like recommendation, not advertisement
- micro-creators with high trust

niche experts with audience loyalty

Consumers can smell transactional influence instantly.

Brands that ignore this are burning money.

The Fall of the Highlight Reel

Social media used to be about documenting the best moments of life.

The Algorithm Didn't Change, People Did

The algorithm still rewards attention. But people reward truth. That's why some influencers with massive audiences are seeing the lowest engagement of their careers, while smaller, more genuine creators continue to grow with far less effort.

Viewers are becoming sharper, more selective, and far less tolerant of manufactured personas.

The Great Unfollow isn't a rejection of social platforms themselves. It's a rejection of being misled, pressured, or performed at.

People aren't abandoning Instagram or TikTok. They're abandoning illusions and choosing creators who feel real, grounded, and trustworthy.

What This Means for Entrepreneurs and Brands

To survive and thrive in this new landscape, brands must adopt a new playbook:

1. Stop buying influence. Start earning it.
Customers trust people who trust the product.

2. Work with creators who use your product off-camera.
Authenticity can't be faked.

3. Think community-first, not platform-first.
Owning your audience wins in the long run.

4. Create content that teaches, not sells.
Trust grows when value grows.

5. Leverage micro and nano creators.
Small voices have deep reach.

6. Prioritize long-term partnerships.
Consistency signals conviction.

7. Encourage messiness.
Human beats polished every time.

The Great Unfollow is not a crisis.

It's a correction.

Consumers are simply demanding what the influencer industry forgot to deliver:

integration of truth, value, and humanity.

The brands and creators that embrace this shift will not only survive the new digital landscape; they'll define it.

Influence isn't disappearing.

It's coming home to the people who actually earned it.

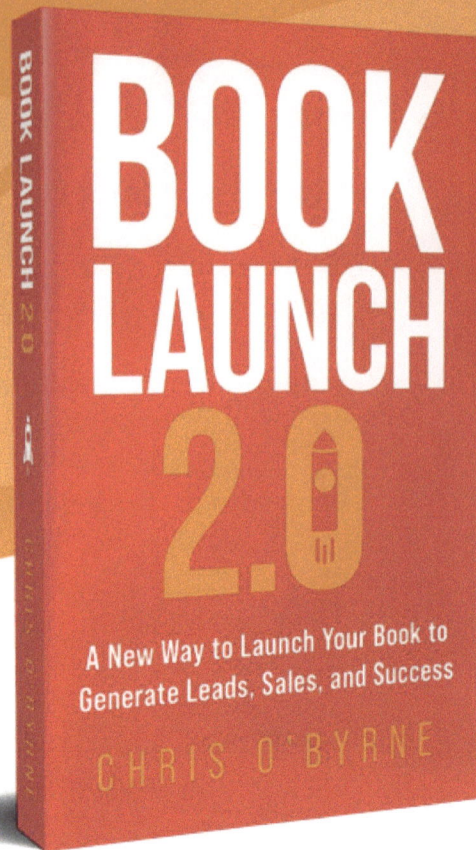

FROGMAN MINDFULNESS

Jon Macaskill
US Navy SEAL Commander (Ret)
Keynote Speaking
One on One Coaching
Mindfulness Teaching
www.frogmanmindfulness.com
757-619-1211

www.ingramcontent.com/pod-product-compliance
Lightning Source LLC
Chambersburg PA
CBHW041703200326
41518CB00002B/169